Dispatches: Turning Points in Theology and Global Crises

Dispatches draws on the legacy of early-twentieth-century theological responses to the crises of the two world wars. During World War II, the *Signposts* (Dacre Press, 1940) series sought to offer an interruption of a theological malaise in the midst of mass violence and destruction. Contributors from that series, including Julian Casserlay, Eric Mascall, and Donald MacKinnon, among others, offered slim volumes that drew from diverse resources and harnessed the apocalyptic political urgency of the dialectical school within the theological grammar of a more traditional Anglo-Catholic Thomism. Similarly, and inspired significantly by MacKinnon's contributions, this present series draws on diverse theological resources in order to offer urgent responses to contemporary crises.

While the title of the series conveys the digest nature of the volumes, the subtitle, *Turning Points*, indicates the apocalyptic urgency of the issues addressed. Yet, there is no prescriptive theological stream within which the tradition is to be re-appropriated by our authors. The goal of the series is to offer a genuinely creative and disruptive theological-ethical *ressourcement* for the church in the present moment. With conceptual agility and faithfulness, this series will provide intelligent and accessible reflections on the shape and form of theological life in the present.

Dispatches will illuminate and explore, creatively and concisely, the implications and relevance of theology for the global crises of late modernity. Our authors have been invited to introduce succinct and provocative arguments intended to provoke dialogue and exchange of ideas, while setting in relief the implications of theology for political and moral life.

Series Editors

Ashley John Moyse (PhD, Newcastle) is the McDonald Postdoctoral Fellow in Christian Ethics and Public Life, Christ Church, Oxford. He has previously served as the Templeton Foundation Postdoctoral Fellow in Theology and Science at Regent College in Vancouver, British Columbia. In addition to his work with Dispatches series, he has authored *Reading Karl Barth, Interrupting Moral Technique, Transforming Biomedical Ethics* (Palgrave, 2015) and coedited several volumes, including *Correlating Sobornost: Conversations Between Karl Barth and the Russian Orthodox Tradition* (Fortress, 2016), *Kenotic Ecclesiology: Select Writings of Donald M. MacKinnon* (Fortress, 2016), and *Treating the Body in Medicine* *and Religion: Jewish, Christian, and Islamic Perspectives* (Routledge, forthcoming).

Scott A. Kirkland (PhD, Newcastle) is the inaugural Postdoctoral Fellow for the Trinity College Theological School, University of Divinity, Melbourne. He is the author of *Into the Far Country: Karl Barth and the Modern Subject* (Fortress, 2016), and co-editor, with Ashley John Moyse and John C. McDowell, of *Correlating Sobornost: Conversations Between Karl Barth and the Russian Orthodox Tradition* (Fortress, 2016) and *Kenotic Ecclesiology: Select Writings of Donald M. MacKinnon* (Fortress, 2016).

Printed Titles

The End Is Not Yet by John W. de Gruchy

Forthcoming Titles

Theology and the Globalized Present by John C. McDowell
Gender Violence Church by Anna Mercedes
The Art of Living for a Technological Age by Ashley John Moyse
Theology, Comedy, Politics by Marcus Pound
Intersectionality, Religion, and Theology by Joerg Rieger

Political Orthodoxies

Political

Orthodoxies

The Unorthodoxies of the Church Coerced

Cyril Hovorun

Fortress Press
Minneapolis

POLITICAL ORTHODOXIES

Cover image: Untitled painting by Yuriy Khimich (1928–2003)

Cover design: Alisha Lofgren

Paperback ISBN: 978-1-5064-3160-4

eBook ISBN: 978-1-5064-5311-8

The paper used in this publication meets the minimum requirements of American National Standard for Information Sciences — Permanence of Paper for Printed Library Materials, ANSI Z329.48-1984.

Manufactured in the U.S.A.

This book was produced using Pressbooks.com, and PDF rendering was done by PrinceXML.

To my colleagues at Sankt Ignatios
Theological Academy

Contents

Acknowledgments

I wrote most of this book during the 2016–2017 academic year at Loyola Marymount University in Los Angeles. It is an outcome of the fellowship program at Huffington Ecumenical Institute, which is affiliated with Loyola Marymount. I am profoundly grateful to the institute and its director at that time, Fr. Nicholas Denysenko. I am thankful to many people at LMU for their support of my studies. The book was finalized during my time as visiting professor at the University of Münster in Germany, where I participated in the Cluster of Excellence "Religions and Politics in Premodern and Modern Cultures." There is also another institution I want to thank, Sankt Ignatios Theological Academy in Sweden, where I was employed for several years before moving to California. Its mission is to provide Eastern Christianity with new patterns of theological education and thinking about the church. This is

a thinking liberated from various unorthodox Orthodoxies. The book is dedicated to the efforts of the dean
of the Academy, Michael Hjälm, and his team, who are
making theological education more genuine and more
relevant to our time.

Introduction

Jesus Christ resisted the temptation of receiving control over the kingdoms of the world (Matt 4:8–10). He declined to participate in the Jewish resistance against the oppressing power of Rome (Matt 22:21). This frustrated many who expected him to play a political role. He instead preached the kingdom of God, which "is not of this world" (John 18:36). Jesus's standpoint regarding political agendas of his time was a new thing (Rev 21:5) in comparison with the theopolitical ethos of antiquity, where there was no religion without politics and vice versa. Separation between the two was unthinkable. Christ made the unthinkable a norm. He introduced a new normal of believing, behaving, and belonging. It can be epitomized in the term *Orthodoxy*, which eventually came to identify Eastern Christianity. Among other new norms, Christian Orthodoxy initially included the imperative of separation between religion and politics and the idea that religion is a matter of free acceptance by an individual, not a public function managed by the state. Upholding this Orthodoxy caused tensions for early Christian communities with Roman society, which perceived the Christian religion as disloyal. Tensions periodically broke into persecutions. Early Christians agreed to pay with their wealth, health, and even their lives for the emancipation of religion from politics.

The situation changed after the conversion of the Roman Empire to Christianity: politics and religion reunited in the single theopolitical body of the Byzantine civilization. In this body, theology often turned political, and politics often expressed itself through theological formulas, producing some premodern forms of political Orthodoxies. In this book, political Orthodoxy is understood as deviation from the original Christian Orthodoxy of separation between religion and politics. It is an unorthodox Orthodoxy.

Several ancient heresies can be interpreted as quasi-religious doctrines featuring strong political agendas. For example, Arianism, the firstborn political Orthodoxy, was delivered immediately after the honeymoon of the church and state. Arianism exaggerated the monarchy of the Father in the Trinity and diminished the Son to creature. It thus legitimized the absolutist monarchy of the Christian emperors, who surpassed their pagan predecessors in accumulating political authority. Two centuries later, another political

Orthodoxy, monothelitism, was designed to repair the imperial mechanism damaged by a civil war and Persian campaigns.[1] Monothelitism saw Jesus Christ as one being with two natures, but one will. This christological model enhanced the will of the emperor over the two "natures" of the Byzantine theocracy—*ekklēsia* and *politeia*. Following the theological model of the single-willed divine Son, the emperor united absolutely the two distinct realms—church and state—under his imperial will. A century later, this led to iconoclasm, which was imposed on the church by the imperial will. Arianism, monothelitism, and iconoclasm constitute premodern instances of political Orthodoxy. The state promoted them as Christian Orthodoxy for political reasons, but the church eventually condemned them as heresies. For all their differences, these heresies commonly featured curtailing the initial Christian momentum toward separation between the ecclesial and political.

Not every political Orthodoxy was declared heresy. Some forms of political impact on Christianity were appropriated by the church and became an intrinsic part of its tradition. Such was, for instance, the principle of hierarchy in the ecclesial orders. The hierarchical principle was imported to Christianity in late antiquity from the Roman political world. It is thus

1. I have studied the political impact on theological doctrines in the late antiquity in Cyril Hovorun, *Will, Action and Freedom: Christological Controversies in the Seventh Century* (Leiden: Brill, 2008), 53–102.

political in its nature. This principle is useful in managing the structures of the church. At the same time, it makes the church more vulnerable to the abuses of hierarchism and stratification. The same applies to the Byzantine symphony model of relations between the church and state. According to this model, the church and state were conflated into a single theopolitical torrent. Theologians like Eusebius of Caesarea (260/265–339/340) presented symphony as a divine gift, but in fact it served political conveniences of the state and church.[2] The model of symphony is an example of political Orthodoxy that is not harmful as such but opened doors to more harmful forms of it, such as coercion.

Most political Orthodoxies explored in this book have been adopted by the church in modern times. Like their ancient predecessors, they can be interpreted as heresies that pretend to be Orthodox but in fact are unorthodox Orthodoxies. Among the most popular modern heresies in the Orthodox world are nationalism (chap. 5), anti-Semitism (chap. 4), and fundamentalism (chap. 3). They claim that they protect Orthodox identity in the modern world. In effect,

---

2. In my previous books on ecclesiology, I studied how the principle of hierarchy led to stratification within the church, and how symphony compromised the self-awareness of the church by blending it with the political consciousness of the Byzantine state. See Cyril Hovorun, *Meta-Ecclesiology: Chronicles on Church Awareness* (New York: Palgrave Macmillan, 2015), 37–68; Cyril Hovorun, *Scaffolds of the Church: Towards Poststructural Ecclesiology* (Eugene, OR: Cascade, 2017), 145–62.

however, they alienate Christians from the apostolic and patristic ethos, and confine the church in the frame of *this* world. Within the confinement of this world, the church easily engages in culture wars, which are political in their nature. Orthodox culture wars are in some regards similar, but they are also different from the culture wars in the West. Some aspects of the Orthodox culture wars are studied in detail in chapter 3 of the book. Like in the West, they are ideological. In contrast to some liberal Western churches, however, Eastern churches often identify themselves with political conservatism and condemn liberalism as heresy. Eastern Christians still prefer monarchy to democracy, strong men with unchecked political power to the rule of law, archaism to modernity, and so on.

Wrestling with political Orthodoxies can be presented in many ways. For instance, it can be rendered as a conflict between Orthodoxy as a predicate of Christianity—Orthodox Christianity—and Orthodoxy as noun. Orthodoxy as a noun in our time primarily means identity. In early Christian times, however, Orthodoxy was one of many qualities of Christianity, functioning as an adjective describing the noun Christianity. It denoted the genuine—Orthodox—way of praying to and believing in the God revealed in Jesus Christ. With the passage of time, Orthodoxy evolved from the way one prayed and believed to the way an individual or a people identify themselves.[3] Such a transformation is not problematic as such, but it becomes a problem when Orthodoxy comes to mean nothing else but identity.

A 2017 study by the Pew Research Center, "Religious Belief and National Belonging in Central and Eastern Europe," to which there are many references throughout the book, articulated these transformations in the terms of believing, behaving, and belonging.[4] Belonging stands here for identity. The Pew study established:

> In the Orthodox countries, there has been an upsurge of religious identity, but levels of religious practice are comparatively low. And Orthodox identity is tightly bound up with national identity, feelings of pride and cultural superiority, support for linkages between national churches and governments, and views of Russia as a bulwark against the West.[5]

All these are elements of political Orthodoxies that we will scrutinize in the book. All of them relate to identity, especially where the latter is divorced from faith (believing) and ethics (behaving). True Christian Orthodoxy is only possible when there is a balance between faith, ethics, and identity. When identity substitutes for faith and ethics, Orthodoxy turns unortho-

---

3. See Cyril Hovorun, "Was Eastern Christianity Always Orthodox?," *The Wheel*, March 2015, 2–8.
4. Pew Research Center, "Religious Belief and National Belonging in Central and Eastern Europe," Pew Reserach Center, May 10, 2017, https://tiny url.com/y9ejlfx9.
5. Pew Research Center, "Religious Belief and National Belonging," 14.

dox. It can lead to violence and even wars. That is how the Russian aggression against Ukraine became possible in 2014. It was preceded by another war, when in 2008 Russia intervened in Georgia. The only wars on the European continent in the beginning of the twenty-first century were waged between Orthodox countries. A century earlier, there were wars between other Orthodox countries: Greece, Bulgaria, and Serbia. The concept of political Orthodoxies will help us explain these outbursts of violence between Orthodox nations (chap. 2).

Modern political Orthodoxies can also be presented as ideologies dressed in the robes of theology. The task of the book is to demarcate between them. This task is not easy. Theology and ideology sometimes look like twins. This is because ideology budded from theology in the beginning of the modern era. Ideology inherited from theology a faithfulness to the unseen and the capacity to indoctrinate masses. The difference between the two is that for theology the unseen is uncreated God, while for ideology, the unseen is the world of ideas confined to the human mind. The former drives masses to God in eternity, and the latter to temporary political and social goals. Modern political Orthodoxies fall in between theology and ideology—they pursue either secular agendas in the name of God or religious agendas by political means. Secularity as the framework of political Orthodoxies is explained in chapter 1 of the book.

If the church can be presented as a body of those who gathered in the name of Jesus (1 Cor 12:12–14; Col 1:18, 24; Eph 5:29), political Orthodoxies are a specific sort of infirmity of this body. They are different, for instance, from the rheumatic disorder of the church's administrative structures. That sort of disorder is caused by weariness of internal organs.[6] The political Orthodoxies I study in this book have a different etiology—like viral infections, churches contract them outside, in public spaces. In the premodern era, the main source of such infections was the state. In our time, it is ideology in most cases.

One of the chronic infections the church has contracted from the state is coercion. Like the principle of hierarchy, it was adopted by Christianity from the Roman world in the period of late antiquity, climaxed during the Middle Ages, and survived the antibiotic treatment of separation between the church and state in the age of reason. Coercion functions as a watershed between two phenomena, which are studied in the book (chap. 1) as frames for modern political Orthodoxies: civil and political religions. The categories of civil and political religions come from the sociology of religion. The difference between them is that civil religion is offered for free acceptance, while political religion is imposed by force. All political Orthodoxies considered in this book constitute parts of either civil

---

6. I studied some internal disorders of ecclesial structures, such as ecclesiocentrism or jurisdictionism, in Hovorun, *Scaffolds of the Church*, 205, 207.

or political religions. Orthodox churches, once on the track of civil religion, easily slide to its relative—political religion. Chapter 2 of the book explores cases of such transition.

Social sciences help explain how modern ideologemes turn to *theologoumena*.[7] The book explores some of them: antimodernism, monarchism, and conservatism (chap. 3). They relate to each other and yet are different. For instance, antimodernism and conservatism together resist the process of the modernization of society. At the same time, the former can completely isolate the church from society, as in the case of fundamentalism. In contrast to antimodernism, conservatism makes the church deeply engaged in sociopolitical processes. For example, when the churches identify themselves with conservatism, they soon find themselves in the trenches of culture wars, as often happens in the United States. When antimodernism and conservatism pair with Christian Orthodoxy, they both downgrade Christianity to ideological schemata. As for monarchism, it is rooted in the imperial past of the Orthodox churches. In the modern context, it is one of the forms of antidemocratic antimodernism. Many Orthodox conservatives express their political preferences in terms of monarchism.

---

7. By *ideologeme* I understand particular beliefs that constitute elements of larger ideological systems. *Theologoumena* are theological opinions, which are not necessarily a part of the church doctrine, but many believe them to be such.

This book pays special attention to anti-Semitism (chap. 4), which is regarded here as a christological heresy. This heresy strips Jesus of his Jewishness, and thus of his real humanity. Anti-Semitism is therefore a form of ancient Docetism, which in the early Christian centuries also denied the real humanity of Jesus. Both heresies undermine the incarnation of God and challenge its salvific effect on humanity. In some contexts, anti-Semitism substitutes the figure of Jesus Christ with the figure of the antichrist—"the man of lawlessness" and "the son of destruction" (2 Thess 2:3)—who will come in the last days to deceive the faithful (1 John 2:18). Although *modern* anti-Semitism looks like an ancient heresy, it is a product of modernity somehow different from "classical," *premodern* anti-Semitism. The latter interpreted Judaism as a religion, while the former interprets it as an ethnicity. Modern ethnic anti-Semitism became an intrinsic part of nationalist ideologies.

The book studies nationalism (chap. 5) as an instance of civil and political religions. Nationalism can be either civil or coercive. It can be also either ethnic or civilizational. In the former case, it helps build nations, and in the latter, it builds empires. The ethnic form of nationalism is an existential threat to empires. All three empires of the past with significant Orthodox populations—Ottoman, Austro-Hungarian, and Russian—collapsed under the pressure of ethnic "civil" nationalism. At its early stage, nationalism in these empires was an inclusive and emancipatory force that fought for the equal political and religious rights of minorities. After minorities managed to depart from empires and established national states, their nationalism often turned toxically exclusive. It mutated from being an advocate of equal rights for nations to the promoter of the superiority of one nation over others. The church participated in both stages of nationalism. In coherence with the first, emancipatory stage, the church downgraded its own hierarchical structures and became more accessible for ordinary people. At the second stage, it contributed to what Philip Gorski calls "political idolatry dressed up as religious orthodoxy."[8]

As a result, almost all Orthodox churches and peoples nowadays are affected by different forms of nationalism. Numbers of nationalists in the "Orthodox" societies are high—they are higher than in the "Catholic" or "Protestant" societies. According to the aforementioned 2017 Pew research, the Orthodox countries in Eastern and Southern Europe were 23 percent more nationalistic than non-Orthodox countries in the same region (68 against 45 percent). Among the champions of nationalism were Greece (89 percent) and Georgia (85 percent). The least nationalistic Orthodox countries, according to the Pew study, were Ukraine (41 percent) and Belarus (42 percent).[9]

8. Philip Gorski, *American Covenant: A History of Civil Religion from the Puritans to the Present* (Princeton: Princeton University Press, 2017), 3.

If one could write a book on all instances of modern political Orthodoxies, the bulky volumes required would be a challenge for any publisher. The scope of this book, therefore, is reduced to a few cases only: Greek, Romanian, and Russian. Many other contexts and issues remain outside this study: the role of the Serbian church in the Yugoslavian wars of 1991–2001 and in the massacre of Muslims in Srebrenica (1995); the collaboration of the Orthodox churches in the Middle East with the regimes of Saddam Hussein and Bashar al-Assad; and the cases of Bulgarian, Ukrainian, Georgian, and many other nationalisms whose addition would make the picture of political Orthodoxies more complete. I leave these cases to other scholars.

It seems that the church cannot get rid of political Orthodoxies altogether: their different forms replace each other but do not go away forever. There is and will always be a penultimate struggle between the gospel's Orthodoxy and the politicized unorthodox Orthodoxy. This war began in the early Christian era and will end in the eschaton. Each generation is called to win a battle for itself, but the war continues on. This book has been written for the post-Soviet and post–Cold War generation as a guide to the political Orthodoxies pertinent to this period.

9. Pew Research Center, "Religious Belief and National Belonging," 13.

1

Secularism, Civil Religion, and Political Religion

Secularism

We will consider various forms of political Orthodoxies through the prism of three concepts: secularism, civil religions, and political religions. These concepts have been elaborated in the frame of social sciences. This does not mean, however, that our analysis of political Orthodoxies will be sociological only. It will also be theological and historical. We will be talking about religious phenomena turning political and vice versa. In this sense, all political Orthodoxies explored in this book are secular phenomena. They became an intrinsic part of various civil and political religions. We will judge them against theological criteria in sociological language.

The first concept that covers modern forms of political Orthodoxies like a canopy is secularism.[1] Secularism can be beneficial for the church, when, for instance, it liberates religion from political obligations. It clears a path for the church to discover the church's true self. In what follows, however, we will concentrate on the negative impact of secularism when it infects the church with ideology. Most forms of political Orthodoxy turn secular even when they want to wrestle with secularism. Before we proceed to analyzing why political Orthodoxies are largely secular, we need to make some terminological distinctions between three related but particular terms: *secularism*, *secular*, and *secularization*. These all refer to a space free from religion; however, their approaches to this space differ. *Secularism* is an ideology and a political agenda that ostracizes religion from the public square with the ultimate goal of exterminating religion altogether. This ideology is usually oppressive to religion. *Secular* describes the character of a political, social, or ecclesial

---

1. See Peter Berger, *The Sacred Canopy. Elements of a Sociological Theory of Religion* (Garden City, NY: Doubleday, 1967).

space. It can be neutral or even beneficial for the church. Finally, *secularization* is an objective social or political process that leads to gradual abandonment of different social domains by religion.

All three terms come from the Latin word *saeculum*, which in Greek is *aeōn* [αἰών]. Both words originally meant "century" or "age." Early Christian writers used the word *saeculum* in application to *this* world as opposed to the eternal world of God, which they often called the "ages of ages" (*saecula saeculorum*; οἱ αἰῶνες τῶν αἰώνων). Augustine, for instance, denoted as *saeculum* the world measured by time.[2] He opposed it to the "city of God," which exceeds any frame of time.

The juxtaposition between *saeculum* and *saecula saeculorum* was elaborated upon in modern sociology of religion. For instance, Charles Taylor in his famous book *A Secular Age* defined as "immanent frame" what the Fathers of the church called *saeculum*. The Taylorean frame became all-embracing in the period of modernity. It has included states, societies, and even some churches. This frame is immanent because it belongs to *this* world. Everything within this frame appears to be trapped in *saeculum* and has very limited access to *saecula saeculorum*. The prevalence of the "immanent frame" over the transcendental divine sphere, *saecula saeculorum*, has become a characteristic feature of modernity, according to Taylor:

2. R. A. Markus, *Saeculum: History and Society in the Theology of St Augustine* (Cambridge: Cambridge University Press, 1970), xxii.

15

> We can come to see the growth of civilization, or moder-
> nity, as synonymous with the laying out of the closed
> immanent frame; within this civilized values develop,
> and a single-minded focus on the human good, aided by
> the fuller and fuller use of scientific reason, permits the
> greatest flourishing possible of human beings.[3]

The immanent framework is thus a characteristic feature of modernity. It differentiates modernity from the
premodern stages of human civilization: antiquity and
Middle Ages. Premodernity related itself to the divine,
saecula saeculorum, while modernity has made even the
divine a part of the secular immanent frame. Modern
churches have not escaped this frame. Some of them
deliberately and consciously embrace secularity, and
some find themselves locked into it while wrestling
against secularism. The more the latter churches fight
against secularism, the deeper they may sink to the
immanent frame of secularity. These churches may
claim that they struggle in the name of God for tran-
scendent goals, but their methods are confined to this
world.

Locked in the immanent frame, both secularism and
anti-secularism turn to ideologies. Ideology is a theology that has been secularized. Politicized religion is
intrinsically ideological. Although ideologies belong to
the post-theological era, they are structurally similar

3. Charles Taylor, *A Secular Age* (Cambridge, MA: Belknap Press of Harvard University Press, 2007), 548.

to theology. Both ideologies and theologies feature ideas that explain visible reality and try to change it according to invisible patterns. Ideologies, like theology: (1) put ideas above the visible world; (2) are eager to subsume or even to sacrifice the visible world to ideas; (3) offer a holistic worldview; (4) easily mobilize masses; and (5) act with the power of a myth.[4] In this sense, ideologies constitute a "secular religion" with its own "priests"—the intellectuals.[5] The difference between ideology and theology, however, is that theological ideas lead a person to the divine, *saecula saeculorum*, while ideological ideas confine masses to the immanent frame of *saeculum*.

Ideology is a product of the process of secularization. It was invented in the beginning of modernity as an alternative to religion and was intended to exercise a religious impact on people's mind and behavior. The French philosopher Antoine Destutt de Tracy (1754–1836), who coined the term "ideology," set *les eléments d'idéologie* ["the elements of ideology"] as foundations for secular epistemology.[6] A faithful follower of the Enlightenment, de Tracy constructed ideology as a way of perceiving the truth without engaging a "religious bias."[7]

---

4. See Daniel Bell, *The End of an Ideology: On the Exhaustion of Political Ideas in the Fifties* (New York: Collier, 1962), 399.
5. See Bell, *End of an Ideology*, 394, 400.
6. This is the title of Destutt de Tracy's main work, *Eléments d'idéologie*, published in five volumes in the period 1801–1815.
7. See Bell, *End of an Ideology*, 394–95.

Almost half a century later, the concept of ideology reemerged in the works of Karl Marx (1818–1883), now itself an object of criticism for bias and distortion of reality. Ideology evolved from the accuser to the accused. Marx, in his work *Die deutsche Ideologie* ["The German Ideology"] (1846),[8] criticized German idealistic philosophy for misrepresenting reality.[9] Marx argued that when the picture of reality is drawn on the basis of ideas alone, a method the idealist philosophers committed themselves to, it leads to false consciousness. The true picture of reality can be drawn only on the canvas of the economic interests of social classes.

While wrestling with idealist ideologies, Marxism gradually turned into an ideology itself. In its Soviet version, it became a totalitarian ideocracy. Fascist movements that came to power on the pretext of fighting against Communism also turned into totalitarian ideologies. Ideologies became blueprints for gigantic projects of social engineering in the twentieth century and ended as bloodbaths with millions of human lives sacrificed to their ideas.

The tragic consequences of the totalitarian ideologies led to the crisis of ideology as a genre. In 1960, Daniel Bell declared that ideologies had completely exhausted themselves.[10] In some senses, he was right,

---

8. See Harald Bluhm, *Karl Marx, Friedrich Engels, Die deutsche Ideologie* (Berlin: Akademie Verlag, 2010).
9. See Wolfgang Thumser, *Kirche im Sozialismus: Geschichte, Bedeutung und Funktion einer ekklesiologischen Formel* [Church in Socialism: History, Meaning, and Function of an Ecclesiological Formula] (Tübingen: J.C.B. Mohr, 1996).

as ideologies had lost their sway over peoples' minds, at least in the West.[11] Postmodernism, which emerged in the beginning of the twentieth century but came to power after World War II, was among the killers of classical ideologies. At the core of postmodernist power, which weakened modernism, was relativism. As it advanced, however, postmodernism gradually turned itself into an ideology.

Both modern and postmodern ideologies contributed to the development of secularism. This concept is different from the concept of secular, as mentioned earlier, and the difference between them is signified by the suffix -ism. This suffix is usually a token of an ideology. Among the founders of secularism as an ideology were David Hume (1711–1776) and Auguste Comte (1798–1857).[12] George Jacob Holyoake (1817–1906), who followed in their footsteps, coined the word *secularist*. In its original meaning, it was synonymous with the words *infidel*, *freethinker*, and *unbeliever*.[13] Holyoake, who publicly propagated and campaigned for atheism,[14] nevertheless distinguished between

10. See Bell, *End of an Ideology*.
11. It took a few decades more before the ideologies bankrupted in the Eastern bloc.
12. See David Hume, *Hume on Religion* (Cleveland, OH: World, 1964); Auguste Comte, *Système de politique positive. Ou traité de sociologie, instituant la religion de l'humanité* [System of Positive Polity] (Bruxelles: Culture et Civilisation, 1969).
13. See Nikki Keddie, "Secularism and Its Discontents," *Daedalus* 132, no. 3 (2003), 14–15.
14. See his pamphlet George Jacob Holyoake, *Principles of Secularism. Briefly Explained* (London: Austin, 1871).

atheism and secularism. Unlike the atheists, who reject the existence of God, the secularists do not necessarily deny God but consider religion irrelevant to modern society. Secularists, according to Holyoake, disregard theories about the unseen and rely only on facts that can be verified empirically.[15] Secularism thus cohered with positivism, a system of thought that became popular in the nineteenth century. It based itself on "positive" scientific data collected from experiment. The positivist epistemology based on experiment rejected the metaphysical method as based on scientifically unverifiable religious experience. Secularism weaponized the positivist method to make a modern person irrelevant or even hostile to religion.

Secularism, philosophically elaborated by thinkers like Hume and Comte and propagated by public activists like Holyoake, was radical. It pursued a complete expulsion of religion from society as a result of the advance of progress. The idea of the radical secularization of society continued into the twentieth century. In the countries of the Communist bloc, which followed Marxist ideology, it took a form of militant campaigns against religion. Western democracies preferred a softer approach of boycotting religion.

Peter Berger (1929–2017) summarized the program of post–WWII Western secularism in his comment for the *New York Times* in 1968: "By the twenty-first cen-

---

15. See Noah Feldman, *Divided by God: America's Church-State Problem—and What We Should Do about It* (New York: Farrar, Straus & Giroux, 2005), 113–14.

tury, religious believers are likely to be found only in small sects, huddled together to resist a worldwide secular culture."[16] By the beginning of the twenty-first century, however, Berger admitted that he was wrong. He instead acknowledged that religion remains pretty much alive in Western society, and secularism has not harmed it.[17]

The ideology of secularism does not give up and has now become what can be called neo-secularism. One of its proponents, Steve Bruce, in his book *Secularization: In Defence of an Unfashionable Theory*,[18] developed an apologetics in the 1960s style of secularism. On the one hand, he advocates for classical theories of secularism, according to which progress makes religion obsolete. On the other hand, he acknowledges the complexity of secularization processes and warns against perceiving them in a linear way. To survive in a society based on the principles of individualism, pluralism, egalitarianism, and rationalism, religion should find "work to do other than relating individuals to the supernatural."[19] In other words, religion should confine itself to the Taylorean "immanent frame."

Some churches appear to have deliberately com-

---

16. "A Bleak Outlook Is Seen for Religion," *New York Times*, February 25, 1968, 3.
17. Peter Berger, ed., *The Desecularization of the World: Resurgent Religion and World Politics* (Grand Rapids: Eerdmans, 1999), 2.
18. Steve Bruce, *Secularization: In Defence of an Unfashionable Theory* (Oxford: Oxford University Press, 2011).
19. Steve Bruce, *God Is Dead: Secularization in the West* (Malden, MA: Blackwell, 2002), 30.

plied with Bruce's recommendations. They have sur-
rendered to the ideology of secularism on its own
terms. As a result, they concentrate on exclusively
social agendas, making long statements on political
issues and keeping their talk centered on God brief.
Other churches have rebelled against secularism; however, their rebellion does not always lead to liberation
from their ideological cage. By opposing the ideology
of secularism, they sometimes develop a different sort
of ideology, another -*ism*: anti-secularism.

The fullest embodiment of anti-secularism is fundamentalism. The term comes from the collection of
leaflets, *The Fundamentals: A Testimony of Truth* published by Evangelical groups in Chicago in the 1910s.[20]
The initial program of these groups argued against biblical criticism and rationalism in matters of faith. It
gradually developed into a broader antimodernist
agenda and spread widely through various denominations in the United States and beyond. World War I
made fundamentalism switch from relatively irenic to
military language. Its vocabulary now included "skir-
mishes," "battles," and "crusades" against modernism.
However, its "battle royal," the Scopes Trial (1925),
brought a Pyrrhic victory that irreparably damaged its
reputation in Western society.

In the 1940s, fundamentalist groups within different
churches built trans-denominational alliances. In the

---

20. R. A. Torrey and A. C. Dixon, *The Fundamentals: A Testimony to the Truth*
(Grand Rapids: Baker, 2008).

1960s, they volunteered for the culture wars. Secularism became their arch-enemy. To wrestle with it, they employed intellectual, social, and media instruments,[21] most of which were secular. This transformed fundamentalism into an effectively secular phenomenon. R. Scott Appleby noticed this paradox of fundamentalism:

> Herein lies a defining irony of fundamentalisms: these self-proclaimed defenders of traditional religion are hardly "traditional" at all. . . . Fundamentalists have little patience for traditionalist or merely conservative believers, who attempt to live within the complex and sometimes ambiguous boundaries of the historic tradition. Fundamentalists, by contrast, are "progressives" in the sense that they seek to mobilize the religious tradition for a specific temporal end (even if the final victory is expected to occur beyond history). Involvement in politics, civil war, liberation movements and social reform is central to the fundamentalist mentality: religion is, or should be, a force for changing the world, bringing it into conformity with the will of God, advancing the divine plan. In this aspiration fundamentalists are little or no different from other "progressive" religious movements for social change and justice.[22]

The ideology of anti-secularism thus cannot escape the immanent frame of modernity. This frame makes the

---

21. See Clark H. Pinnock, *Biblical Revelation: The Foundation of Christian Theology* (Chicago: Moody, 1971), x.
22. R. Scott Appleby, "Fundamentalisms," in *A Companion to Contemporary Political Philosophy*, ed. Robert E. Goodin, Philip Pettit, and Thomas W. Pogge (Malden, MA: Wiley Blackwell, 2007), 1:407.

ideologies of secularism and anti-secularism similar to each other. In this frame, both ideologies contribute to the social phenomena that we will consider next: social and political religions.

Civil Religion

The term *civil religion* was coined at the dawn of the modern era by Jean-Jacques Rousseau (1712–1778). Rousseau made the concept of "civil religion" a keystone of his theory of social contract. He envisaged it as a glue to keep individuals within the confines of a republican state.[23] Civil religion, to him, counterbalanced the social contract and blocked the unavoidable centrifugal social forces that were released by the contract. Civil religion in Rousseau's understanding was different from any traditional religion and consisted of a set of basic ethical norms. It was to be upheld publicly, while citizens were allowed to keep their traditional religiosity in private.[24] Rousseau regarded civil religion as intrinsically moralistic; he reduced metaphysics to ethics.

The term *civil religion* migrated from the lexicon of the French Enlightenment to the vocabulary of modern scholarship through the works of the American

23. See Jean-Jacques Rousseau, *The Essential Rousseau: The Social Contract, Discourse on the Origin of Inequality, Discourse on the Arts and Sciences, The Creed of a Savoyard Priest*, trans. Lowell Bair (New York: Penguin, 1975), 17, 20, 107–8, 110.
24. See Rousseau, *Essential Rousseau*, 110–12.

sociologist of religion Robert N. Bellah (1927–2013). Bellah described the political culture in the United States as an "American civil religion." For him, it consisted of "beliefs, symbols, and rituals with respect to sacred things and institutionalized in a collectivity. This religion—there seems to be no other word for it—while . . . sharing much in common with Christianity . . . served as a genuine vehicle of national religious self-understanding."[25] Bellah identified civil religion as a "myth" that underpins the self-awareness of a new nation.[26] This religion exists in parallel to traditional religions and has "its own seriousness and integrity."[27] The concept of "American civil religion" became so popular that Bellah published a number of books on this subject.[28] It also caused heated debates, which eventually urged Bellah to abandon the term.[29]

A disciple of Bellah, Philip Gorski, rehabilitated and rectified the concept of civil religion as the core of the *Pax Americana*. The American civil religion, according to Gorski, is a healthy via media between the extremities of nationalism and secularism:

---

25. Robert N. Bellah, "Civil Religion in America," *Daedalus* 96, no. 1 (1967), 8.
26. Robert N. Bellah, *The Broken Covenant: American Civil Religion in Time of Trial* (Chicago: University of Chicago Press, 1992), 3.
27. Bellah, "Civil Religion in America," 1.
28. Robert N. Bellah, *Beyond Belief: Essays on Religion in a Post-Traditional World* (New York: Harper & Row, 1970); Robert N. Bellah and Phillip Hammond, *Varieties of Civil Religion* (San Francisco: Harper & Row, 1980); Bellah, *Broken Covenant.*
29. See Robert N. Bellah, "Comment: Twenty Years after Bellah: Whatever Happened to American Civil Religion?," *Sociological Analysis* 50, no. 2 (1989), 147.

On the right-hand side we find *Religious Nationalism*, a red-hued canvas in heavy oils, filled with the blood and fire of war and Apocalypse, and replete with battle scenes in which the forces of good and evil square off on land, on sea, and in the air. It is a fantasy scene, filled with supernatural creatures—and vain hopes that justice and peace can be achieved through violence and bloodshed. On the left-hand side hangs *Radical Secularism*, a blue-toned watercolor in cheerful pastels that portrays a congeries of disconnected individuals pursuing their own private interests and pleasures without any especial regard for one another. It is a Utopian tableau, which paints over human evil and vulnerability. Finally, in the middle, we have *Civil Religion*, a panoramic portrait of a diverse people marching together through time toward a Promised Land across landscapes both light and dark. It is hopeful without being fantastical, and progressive without being naïvely optimistic.[30]

Jaroslav Pelikan's (1923–2006) perspective on American civil religion is particularly interesting for our analysis here. In his *Interpreting the Bible and the Constitution*, he renders the American political culture as typologically similar to the Christian tradition. Pelikan applies his analysis of the evolution of the Christian doctrine to the American religious "tradition."[31]

---

30. Philip Gorski, *American Covenant: A History of Civil Religion from the Puritans to the Present* (Princeton: Princeton University Press, 2017), 34–35.
31. See Jaroslav Pelikan, *Interpreting the Bible and the Constitution* (New Haven: Yale University Press, 2004), 115.

According to Pelikan, the American Constitution should be considered, in the terms of civil religion, as an "American Scripture." He argues that other foundational texts, such as the Declaration of Independence or Gettysburg Address, do not bear the same "revealing" power.[32] Pelikan also identifies the "interpretive communities" that transformed the "Scripture" to a "tradition." The most important interpretative community for him are judges "with their robes"—a "hierarchy" of this religion.[33]

In tune with Pelikan's thought, Michael Angrosino characterizes George Washington as "the quasi-divine embodiment of American virtue."[34] He is both a "secular saint" of a new religion and its patriarch.[35] Abraham Lincoln, who shed blood "for his people, sanctifying the very ground that had so recently been saturated with the blood of fratricides,"[36] plays an even more religious role. American civil religion also discloses the original sin of the American nation—slavery, as Barack Obama stated in his "race speech" in 2008.[37]

32. Pelikan, *Interpreting the Bible*, 18–21.
33. Pelikan, *Interpreting the Bible*, 22.
34. Michael Angrosino, "Civil Religion Redux," *Anthropological Quarterly* 75, no. 2 (2002), 251.
35. Angrosino, "Civil Religion Redux," 250.
36. Angrosino, "Civil Religion Redux," 251.
37. "Barack Obama's Speech on Race," *New York Times*, March 18, 2008, https://tinyurl.com/2vwwyd.

Political Religion

Although the term *civil religion* was coined on the European Continent, it became applicable primarily in the American context. Another European concept, that of political religion, came to denote primarily Continental phenomena. As a concept, it was introduced to define political developments in Europe during the twentieth century. Emilio Gentile, an Italian student of European political religions, defined them as

> a type of religion which sacralises an ideology, a movement or a political regime through the deification of a secular entity transfigured into myth, considering it the primary and indisputable source of the meaning and the ultimate aim of human existence on earth.[38]

Continental political religions were in effect modifications of secular ideologies.[39] Ideologies had emerged through the rejection of religion. Their reconciliation with religion produced political religions. Political quasi-religions consist of quasi-theological language and quasi-liturgical cults; they persuade people to uphold political tenets as if they were theological doctrines.

38. Emilio Gentile, "Fascism, Totalitarianism and Political Religion: Definitions and Critical Reflections on Criticism of an Interpretation," in *Fascism, Totalitarianism and Political Religion*, ed. Roger Griffin (London: Routledge, 2005), 34.
39. See Jürgen Moltmann, "Covenant or Leviathan? Political Theology for Modern Times," *Scottish Journal of Theology* 47, no. 1 (1994), 36.

As a term, *political religion* was coined in the nineteenth century. A philosopher from the Hegelian school, Moses Hess (1812–1875), used the term *politische Religion* ["political religion"] to define a religious zeal for social change.[40] Hess described this religion as non-institutional. He wanted this religion to replace traditional religions. His desire was fulfilled in the twentieth century, although he probably would have disliked the results of his wishes.

Bolshevism, fascism, and Nazism were identified as "political religions" in the early 1930s. In 1932, an Austrian writer, Franz Werfel (1890–1945), defined these three major ideologies of his time as quasi-religions. German political philosopher Eric Voegelin (1901–1985), who later emigrated to the United States, titled his 1938 book with this phrase from Hess: *Die politischen Religionen* ["The Political Religions"].[41]

While the concept of civil religion goes back to French republicanism, the concept of political religion traces its origins to German idealism. Georg Wilhelm Friedrich Hegel (1770–1831), due to his concept of state, is considered one of its founders.[42] State, for Hegel, is a "divine" institution that features "majesty and absolute authority." It is an embodiment of the

40. Moses Hess, *Die heilige Geschichte der Menschheit* [The Sacred History of Humanity] (Stuttgart: Hallberger, 1837), 334.
41. Eric Voegelin, *Die politischen Religionen* (Stockholm: Bermann-Fischer Verlag, 1939).
42. See A. James Gregor, *Totalitarianism and Political Religion: An Intellectual History* (Stanford: Stanford University Press, 2012), 16.

"divine will, in the sense that it is Mind present on earth, unfolding itself to be the actual shape and organization of a world."[43] Hegel's understanding of "political religion" can be summarized in the words of A. James Gregor: "Hegel sacralized the State, made History its medium, and human beings its instruments."[44] This definition can be seen as the bottom line of the Continental political religions in the twentieth century.

Ludwig Feuerbach (1804–1872) downgraded Hegelian theology to anthropology and thus locked it into the "immanent frame." His philosophy made man the unique, universal, and highest object of philosophy.[45] The next steps in the evolution of the German political religion were made by Friedrich Engels (1820–1895) and Karl Marx (1818–1883). Engels, who was raised a pious Christian, sublimated his religious sentiments to social change. He called this change a "true religion" and differentiated it from traditional forms of religion.[46] Marx reduced the religion of social change to economics, which remains a *deus ex machina* in some modern doctrines descending from Marxism. Historical materialism became the creed of the Marxist

43. Georg Wilhelm Friedrich Hegel, *Hegel's Philosophy of Right*, ed. Sir Thomas Malcolm Knox (Oxford: Oxford University Press, 2015), §§258, 270.
44. Gregor, *Totalitarianism and Political Religion*, 24.
45. Ludwig Feuerbach, *Principles of the Philosophy of the Future* (Indianapolis: Hackett, 1992), §54.
46. Friedrich Engels, "Schelling and Revolution: Critique of the Latest Attempt of Reaction against the Free Philosophy," in Karl Marx and Friedrich Engels, *Collected Works* (New York: International, 1976), 2:239.

"religion," which, in Gregor's judgment, can be considered the first complete version of "political religion."[47]

The religious nature of Marxism was explored in detail by Nikolai Berdyaev (1874–1948). In his essay "Socialism as Religion" (1906), he distinguishes between two kinds of socialism: one that cares about daily needs of people, and one that functions in the capacity of religion. Berdyaev believed that the Marxist religion is diabolic because it casts away God and threatens human personality.[48]

The Soviet regime fulfilled the Berdyaev's prediction. The founder of the Soviet state, Vladimir Lenin (1870–1924), became the "theologian-in-chief" and the "archpriest" of violent Soviet political religion. The initial Hegelian belief in truth being revealed through history mutated into Lenin's imperative to "put against the wall and shoot"[49] everyone who disagreed with his own interpretation of history. Leninism, and later Stalinism, became particularly violent denominations of Marxist political religion.

Fascism developed in counterposition to communism. While communism featured a universalist take on history, fascism favored the historical particularism

47. Gregor, *Totalitarianism and Political Religion*, 86.
48. Nikolai Berdyaev, "Sotsializm kak religiya" [Socialism as Religion], *Voprosy filosofii i psikhologii* [Issues of Philosophy and Psychology] 85, no. 5 (1906), 511–12.
49. V.I. Lenin, *Polnoye sobraniye sochineniy* [Complete Collection of Works] (Moscow: Izdatel'stvo politicheskoy literatury [Political Literature Press], 1970), 45:90.

associated with a national state. The fascist attitude toward established religion also differed from the communist perspective. Communism regarded it as the "opium of people,"[50] while fascism pretended to protect religion. The fascist take on religion, nevertheless, was idiosyncratic. Religion was useful only insofar as it served the "deity" of the state.[51] However, because no established religion considered the state a deity, fascism was destined to clash with the church and to produce a substitute for religion as such. It is no coincidence that Benito Mussolini (1883–1945) interpreted his fascist movement as a sort of "ecclesia."[52]

Nazism was similar to fascism; both were based on nationalistic ideology. There was, however, a difference between them. In contrast to Italian fascism, German Nazism constructed the idea of its own nation by deconstructing the idea of nation for other people, primarily Jews. Nazism relied on the concept of race, which is a modification of the concept of nation.

The roots of Nazism, just like the roots of communism, can be traced back to German idealistic philosophy. Hitler, for example, relied on Hegel's appreciation of a strong state and Fichte's belief in German exceptionalism.[53] He acknowledged that he read a lot

50. Karl Marx and Friedrich Engels, *On Religion* (Mineola, NY: Dover, 2008), 42.
51. See Gentile, "Fascism, Totalitarianism and Political Religion," 55.
52. See Simonetta Falasca-Zamponi, *Fascist Spectacle: The Aesthetics of Power in Mussolini's Italy* (Berkeley: University of California Press, 2008), 43.
53. Yvonne Sherratt, *Hitler's Philosophers* (New Haven: Yale University Press, 2014), 22.

of Arthur Schopenhauer in the trenches of the Great War: "I carried Schopenhauer's works with me throughout the whole of the First World War. From him I learned a great deal."[54] Schopenhauer's idea that the salvation of a nation can be reached through a denial of the will to live, became particularly formative for Nazis.

In addition to common philosophical roots, communism and Nazism were both totalitarian and constructed on the hatred of particular social groups: the bourgeoisie in the case of communism, and the Jews in the case of Nazism. In mobilizing masses on hatred of social groups, communist ideology led, and Nazism followed. Stalin's Russia was in many regards a prototype for Hitler's Germany. As Ernst Nolte noticed, "The Gulag Archipelago is more original than Auschwitz."[55]

Nazi ideology developed with significant input from the Russians who had fled to Germany after the Bolshevik revolution.[56] The Russian "White" immigration

---

54. Adolf Hitler, *Hitler's Table Talk, Hitler's Conversations Recorded by Martin Bormann*, introduced by Hugh Trevor-Roper (Oxford: Oxford University Press, 1988), 20.

55. Ernst Nolte, *Der eurupäische Bürgerkrieg 1917-1945: Nationalsozialismus und Bolschewismus* [The European Civil War 1917–1945: National Socialism and Bolshevism] (Frankfurt: Propyläen, 1989), 15.

56. One of the first scholars who established connection between Russian monarchism and German National Socialism was Walter Laqueur, *Russia and Germany: A Century of Conflict* (London: Weidenfeld & Nicolson, 1965). See also the fundamental study by Michael Kellogg, *The Russian Roots of Nazism: White Émigrés and the Making of National Socialism, 1917-1945* (Cambridge: Cambridge University Press, 2008). There are also Russian scholars who support this thesis, such as David Raskin and Rafaïl Ganelin (Rafaïl Ganelin, "Ot cher-

(as opposite to the Soviet "Reds") to Germany brought with it an ideology that featured monarchism, imperialism, and anti-Semitism. This ideology was profoundly anti-communist, which made it coherent with Nazism: both Nazis and Russian "White" immigrants hated the Soviet regime. This coherence can be noticed in many writings by the Russian immigrants in Germany, including one of the most prolific thinker among them, Ivan Ilyin (1883–1954).[57]

One of the most important channels of the Russian influence on the formation of Nazism was the think-tank *Aufbau* ("Reconstruction," full name *Aufbau: Wirtschafts-politische Vereinigung für den Osten* ["Reconstruction: Economic-Political Organization for the East"]), which was established in Munich by the "White" immigrants. They followed the model of the "Black Hundred."[58] Hitler came in touch with this group in 1920,[59] after which the group made many contributions to his cause. One of *Aufbau's* members, Alfred Rosenberg (1893–1946), became a chief ideologue of the National Socialist German Workers' Party (NSDAP). Max von Scheubner-Richter (1884–1923), who was killed during the Beer Hall Putsch, became

nosotenstva k fashizmu" [From the Black Hundred Movement to Fascism], in *Pamyati Nikolaya Girenko* [In Memoriam of Nikolay Girenko] (St. Petersburg: МАЭ РАН, 2005), 243–72.

57. See especially his article "National Socialism: A New Spirit," *Vozrozhdeniye* [Renaissance], May 17, 1933, where he dismisses criticism of Nazism as biased and shortsighted.

58. See Ilyin, "National Socialism," 263.

59. Kellogg, *Russian Roots of Nazism*, 1.

a model of Nazi martyrdom. Pyotr Shabelsky-Bork (1893–1952) brought to Germany the *Protocols of the Elders of Zion*—a chief text in Nazi anti-Semitic propaganda.[60] Russian imperial anti-Semitism became one of the most important sources of Nazi anti-Semitism.

"White" Russian anti-Semitism can be summarized as follows: Jews are enemies of Christians. Because of this enmity, Jews want to destroy Christian states, including the most prominent of them—the Orthodox Russian empire—and to establish their rule. This is the rule of the apocalyptic antichrist described in the Scriptures. Jews managed to achieve their goals in Soviet Russia. The Bolshevik revolution in October 1917 was a great success of the Jewish conspiracy against Christian civilization. Now, through their materialist ideology (Marxism), the Jews threaten the entirety of Christian civilization, which always prioritized the principles of spirituality. Germany, as a country whose historical mission is to promote *der Geist* ["the spirit"], is the top target. For this reason, Germany and Russia should be together *über alles* ["above all"].[61] The political programs of the Russian "White" monarchists and German social nationalists thus came to agree on "an anti-Entente (Britain and France), anti-Weimar Republic, anti-Bolshevik, and anti-Semitic struggle."[62]

60. Members of *Aufbau* also contributed money to the NSDAP at its early stage. See Kellogg, *Russian Roots of Nazism*, 1.
61. See Kellogg, *Russian Roots of Nazism*, 15.

The "White" Russians and the "black" Germans concurred in opposing the ideological platform of the "Red" Russians. Still, there was a striking similarity in the Bolshevik and Nazi methods of achieving their goals, however different those might be. Both used concentration camps to confine and exterminate social groups they deemed "enemies of people": bourgeoisie, clergy, and other non-proletarian classes in the former case; Jews, Gypsies, and some other "non-Aryan" ethnicities in the latter case. They also applied starvation as a method of mass extermination. In the early 1930s, Stalin decided to break the backbone of the peasantry, who, he believed, impeded the advance of the proletarian revolution. He created conditions for an artificial famine, *Holodomor*, which affected mostly the central and eastern regions of Ukraine.[63] According to an estimate from the Ukrainian Institute of National Memory, the Ukrainian famine claimed around 4.5 million lives.[64] Stalin's methods of artificial famine were later adopted by Hitler, who sought to solve the Jewish and the Eastern "questions."[65]

Regardless of their ideological antagonisms, Russian monarchists, Soviet communists, Italian fascists, and

---

62. Kellogg, *Russian Roots of Nazism*, 1.
63. See Anne Applebaum, *Red Famine: Stalin's War on Ukraine* (New York: Doubleday, 2017).
64. Ukrainian Institute of National Memory, accessed April 22, 2018, https://tinyurl.com/y8qntlnl.
65. See Timothy Snyder, *Bloodlands: Europe Between Hitler and Stalin* (New York: Basic Books, 2010), 20.

German Nazis commonly favored collectivism over individualism. They also commonly believed in the superiority of the state over an individuum. The only difference between them was their vision for what kind of state should contain individuals. For the "Whites," it was Russian monarchy with the tsar on top of it. For the "Reds," it was the dictatorship of the proletariat. For the fascists, it was *lo stato corporativo* ["the corporate state"] envisaged by Mussolini.[66] For the Nazis, it was the Third German Reich. The state for all of them was the ultimate authority and value, a "Zeus" in the pantheon of their political religions.

Imposing collectivism upon individuals requires strong leadership. This constitutes one of the paradoxes of totalitarian political religions: they begin as populist movements with wide appeal to "simple people." In the end, however, to implement their programs, they come to call for a leader. All political religions in the first half of the twentieth century had leaders with very similar attitude to their political authority: "вождь" Stalin in the Soviet Union, *il duce* Mussolini in Italy, *der Führer* Hitler in Germany, ὁ Ἀρχηγός Metaxas in Greece, *Conducător* Antonescu in Romania, and so on. This attitude, to use the words of Hegel, who underpinned it in his philosophy, trampled "down many an innocent flower" and crushed "to

---

66. Benito Mussolini, *Lo stato corprativo* [The Corporate State], 2nd ed. (Firenze: Vallecchi, 1938).

pieces many an object in its path."[67] In other words, at the core of these figures' leadership was coercion.

Coercion

Political religion and civil religion are similar in many regards: both observe sacred calendars, have public rituals performed by "priests," venerate "prophets" and "martyrs," believe in a "redemption," and have "eschatological" expectations. There is also a significant difference between them: while civil religion inspires people to sacrifice themselves to achieve its eschatological goals, political religion sacrifices other people without their consent. One characteristic feature of political religion is its use of propaganda and coercion to force people to subscribe to its credo. Civil religion may also manipulate public opinion, but it is not coercive. Unlike political religion, it does not apply force to make people believe. People are *encouraged* to freely subscribe to civil religion, and they are *forced* to adhere to political religion. Coercion is a key article in the credo of any political religion.

Coercion is older than any civil or political religion. It is also one of the most ancient political Orthodoxies. Unlike Arianism or iconoclasm, however, it was not condemned as heresy. Moreover, it was often used by

---

67. G. W. F. Hegel, *The Philosophy of History*, trans. J. Sibree (New York: Colonial, 1900), 32.

the state, and accepted by the church, to enforce Nicaean, Chalcedonian, and other Orthodoxies.

Coercion was introduced to the Christian church when Christianity allied with the Roman state. *Imperium Romanorum* not only encouraged coercion but was coercive by its very nature.[68] This nature grew from the martial foundations of the Roman political system. Coercion arranged both the public and private lives of Romans, including their religious beliefs. In the Roman world, religion was never a private matter but always a public function. The state reserved the right to interfere in the religious life of its subjects. Moreover, it considered this life accountable to the state in the same way as, for example, taxation or military service. Through their religion, people demonstrated their loyalty to the state and their commitment to common political causes. Christians during the first three centuries of Christianity were regarded nonloyal subjects for their refusal to participate in public cults. Such behavior was interpreted as an act of disloyalty or even high treason.

Christians had developed a different understanding from the Romans of what religion should be—not a public cult, but an intimate discipleship built on personal relationships and free reception. Christ did not force anyone to follow him. He *called* individuals to join him and waited for *response*. This ethos, based on

68. See Martin Edward Foulkes, "Empire of Coercion: Rome, Its Ruler and His Soldiers," PhD thesis, University of Durham, 2005.

call-response and the rejection of coercion, appeared in the self-identification of Jesus's followers as *ekklēsia*. This word derives from ἐχ-χαλέω—"to be called out." To become a member of the Christian church, *ekklēsia*, meant to develop a relationship with God based on free acceptance and personal response to God's call, not on coercion enforced by the state.

The conversion of the empire to Christianity blurred the clear line of demarcation between the gentile practices of coercion and the Christian freedom-based faith. The church faced a dilemma between the quantity and quality of its membership. Coercion would deliver quantity: more people would join the church, and fewer schisms would occur in the process of their assimilation into the Christian community. In this case, however, the quality of conversion would be compromised. Such quality can be secured only through "hearing" (Rom 10:17), that is, by non-coercive acceptance of faith. There was also a dilemma of double standards: the church, by applying coercion, would adopt the same practices from which it had suffered during persecutions only a few decades earlier.

The symbiosis of the Christian church and the Roman state led to a schizophrenic situation. On the one hand, coercion became a common practice, especially in big cities with political significance. On the other hand, personal relationship with God continued to be cultivated in remote areas where monastic communities were established. Early monasteries became sanctuaries of freedom where Christians could perfect their personal relationship with God in non-coercive ways.

Ambivalence in the practices of coercion in the period of late antiquity can be best illustrated by the attitude of Augustine (354–430). He faced the "Donatist schism" in his native North Africa. The Donatists were a group of Christians who differed from the rest of the church in questions not of doctrine but rather of morality. Today we would probably call them "conservatives" or even "fundamentalists," as they insisted on a stricter moral code and fewer compromises with the world. Their rigor pushed them to get away from the rest of the church and to establish their own network of communities and hierarchy.

As a newly ordained priest, Augustine opposed the practice of coercion toward dissenters. He encouraged local political authorities to use "the most gentle means" against them.[69] He insisted that no one "should against his will be coerced into the Catholic communion."[70] In a few years, however, he reversed his standpoint and fully endorsed emperor Theodosius (347–395) in suppressing paganism in North Africa.[71] He also encouraged local magistrates to force the Donatists to join the Catholic church.[72] Augustine

---

69. In John R. Bowlin, "Augustine on Justifying Coercion," *Annual of the Society of Christian Ethics* 17 (1997): 52.
70. Augustine, *Ep.* 34.1.
71. Augustine, *Sermo* 62.18.
72. Augustine, *Second Letter to Petilianus* 2.

acknowledged that his earlier attitude to the issue was wrong and tried to explain why he had arrived at necessity of coercion: "And truly, at this time, such coercion displeased me because I had not yet learned either how much evil their [Donatists'] impunity would dare or to what extent the application of discipline could bring about their improvement."[73]

Augustine did not introduce coercion to the church—he tried to make theological sense out of it. As Brent Shaw has demonstrated, coercion in the time of Augustine was already standard in church practices.[74] However, coercion soon fired back at the church: the state came to interpret its mission to protect doctrine as right to interfere in matters of faith. The theological crises in the seventh to ninth centuries, including monothelitism and iconoclasm, were caused by the coercive interference of the state.

Such intrusion of the state into matters of faith was met with opposition. For instance, Maximus the Confessor (d. 662) rejected the interventions of the state and was exiled as a result.[75] Maximus also argued against the forceful conversion.[76] In this, he followed the early Christian ethos of freedom of conscience,

73. *Retractions* 2.31.5, in Mary Inez Bogan, *Augustine: The Retractions* (Washington, DC: Catholic University of America Press, 1968), 129.
74. Brent D. Shaw, *Sacred Violence: African Christians and Sectarian Hatred in the Age of Augustine* (Cambridge: Cambridge University Press, 2011), 575.
75. See Pauline Allen and Neil Bronwen, *Maximus the Confessor and His Companions: Documents From Exile* (Oxford: Oxford University Press, 2002), 57.
76. See Andrew Louth, *Greek East and Latin West: The Church, AD 681–1071* (Crestwood, NY: St. Vladimir's Seminary Press, 2007), 138.

which became compromised by the symphonic relationship between the church and the state. Even more radically, coercion was rejected by John Chrysostom (d. 407),[77] who insisted that "to put a heretic to death is an unpardonable crime."[78]

Despite voices such as Maximus's or Chrysostom's, the church in both the East and the West eventually yielded to the practices and theories of coercion, which became an essential feature of the ecclesial ethos through late antiquity and the Middle Ages. The situation did not change even during the Reformation. Protestant churches continued to regard the state as insurer of piety for their members.[79] Johannes Eisermann (Ferrarius, c. 1485–1558), a famous Protestant lawyer from the circle of Philipp Melanchthon (1497–1560) who made a significant contribution to the new legal model of the relationship of the Protestant churches with the local political authorities,[80] advocated for coercion. He particularly stressed the role of princes in securing piety of their subjects: a Christian prince must "direct his office and instructions towards subjects and relatives becoming pious."[81] Severe forms

---

77. See Georges Florovsky, *The Collected Works*, trans. Catherine Edmunds (Vaduz: Büchervertriebsanstalt, 1987), 7:247.

78. Chrysostom, *In Matt.* 46.1.

79. See the study by Thomas Simon in Sigrid Müller and Cornelia Schweiger, eds., *Between Creativity and Norm-Making: Tensions in the Later Middle Ages and the Early Modern Era* (Leiden: Brill, 2013), 241–52.

80. See John Witte, *Law and Protestantism: The Legal Teachings of the Lutheran Reformation* (Cambridge: Cambridge University Press, 2002), 141–53.

81. In Müller and Schweiger, *Between Creativity and Norm-Making*, 247.

of coercion were also practiced in non-conformist theocracies in Europe and America.

Only the process of secularization, initiated in the early modernity, eventually liberated the church from the theories and practices of coercion. Through secularization, the church was deprived of the state's support in exercising coercion. Even when the church wanted to practice coercion, it could not afford to do so. The advance of pluralistic societies also forced the church to reject coercion; there is no way for the church to apply coercion in a pluralistic setting. Last but not least, advances in understanding of human personality and freedom, and their fundamental importance for functioning of modern political systems based on free consent of citizens, placed coercion to the category of unacceptable means of persuasion.[82]

Stigmatization of coercion in secular societies has made coercion unacceptable from a theological perspective. Miroslav Volf has called coercive faith "a seriously malfunctioning faith."[83] Ostracizing coercion from modern society helped the church to rediscover its own distinct way of handling faith—not through compulsion but through dialogue and pursuit. Just as the Roman environment caused the church in late antiquity to accept coercive instruments, so the mod-

---

82. See Jan-Willem van der Rijt, *The Importance of Assent: A Theory of Coercion and Dignity* (Dordrecht: Springer, 2012), 33–34.
83. Miroslav Volf, *A Public Faith: How Followers of Christ Should Serve the Common Good* (Grand Rapids: Brazos, 2011), xvi.

ern sociopolitical environment helps it to get rid of them and to appreciate the means of communication of faith provisioned by the gospel. Modernity, thus, has neutralized some forms of political Orthodoxy that had emerged in the period of antiquity and flourished in the Middle Ages. The ancient practices of forcing someone to religious assent are no longer normal.

Nevertheless, the ancient political Orthodoxy, coercion, did not disappear altogether. It was reincarnated in the new forms of political Orthodoxy—ideology and political religion. As it was demonstrated earlier, ideology became a blueprint for modern civil and political religions. Most civil religions flourished in the nineteenth century, and some of them turned to political religions in the twentieth century. Coercion constitutes the line of demarcation between these two political phenomena. This line, however, was often trespassed by particular Orthodox churches.

2

How Civil Religion Becomes Political Religion: Greece, Romania, and Russia

From the perspective of Christian Orthodoxy, both civil and political religions are forms of politicized religion. Both are unorthodox Orthodoxies, though to a different degree. Political religion is more politicized and less Orthodox than civil religion. Civil religion often paves the way for coercive political religion. This certainly proved true in many Eastern Christian societies, where civil religion opened doors for political religion. We will examine this unfortunate tendency by studying three cases: Greece, Romania, and Russia.

The Greek Case

Greek civil religion is prototypical in the world of Eastern Christianity and archetypal for many Orthodox countries, especially in the Balkans. A product of the Enlightenment, Greek civil religion can also be called a Balkan civil religion. Despite its roots in secularism, it was not anticlerical. Moreover, it was constructed with significant input from clergy and hierarchs. Its main goal was to pursue emancipation from Ottoman rule. Balkan civil religion evolved from a hope for political liberation to making nation a sacred institute. It is based on the constructed narratives of the past—often imagined ones.

Greek civil religion constructed the modern Greek nation by stitching together all the historical periods of Greek history. The author of the modern Greek national narrative, Konstantinos Paparrigopoulos (1815–1891), argued for consistent Hellenism from classical antiquity, through the Byzantine period, up to the Neo-Hellenic state. For him, Hellenism had many historical faces but always remained the same body.[1] This idea, which seems self-evident in our day, was a

---

1. See Antonis Liakos, "Hellenism and the Making of Modern Greece," in Kate-

novelty to the Greeks in the nineteenth century. It correlates with the Christian doctrine of the triune God: just as one God is in three hypostases, so the same Hellenism historically manifested itself through the "hypostases" of classical antiquity, Byzantium, and the free Greek state liberated from the Turkish yoke. This trinitarian metaphor became foundational for Greek civil religion.

The most sacred event of this religion was the liberating revolution of 1821. To be received by people as sacred, its events were aligned with the traditional church calendar. According to the narrative of Greek civil religion, the Metropolitan of Old Patres Germanos (1771–1826) blessed the flag of the Greek revolution on the feast of the Annunciation, March 25. This narrative is not necessarily historically correct, but it functions in the capacity of the civil "holy tradition." The feast of the Annunciation became the most important one in the sacred hemerologion—the list of feasts—of Greek civil religion. It is celebrated as a state holiday, and many Greeks, including those who do not believe in God, attend the celebrations.

Metropolitan Germanos is one of the key figures in the hagiologion—the list of "saints"—of the Greek civil religion. This hagiologion also includes other hierarchs, clergy, and even politicians. Among them are the so-called ethnomartyrs—those church figures who

rina Zacharia, ed., *Hellenisms: Culture, Identity, and Ethnicity from Antiquity to Modernity* (Aldershot: Ashgate, 2008), 211.

sacrificed their lives for the liberation of the Greek nation: the Patriarch of Constantinople Grigorios V, who was hung by the Ottomans as a scapegoat for the revolution of 1821; Metropolitan of Smyrna Chrysostomos, who was murdered by the Turkish rioters in 1922 after the failed Greek military campaign in Asia Minor; and others. One of the venerated figures of Greek civil religion, Athanasios Diakos (1788–1821), was a hierodeacon—a monk in the rank of deacon. His clerical status did not impede him from becoming a rebel against the Ottomans (*kleftis* [κλέφτης], or thief). In the terms of civil religion, these two capacities of Athanasios—a clergyman and a *kleftis*—combine smoothly, even though they are hardly compatible in the terms of a traditional religion. Ioannis Kapodistrias (1776–1831), the first head of the independent Greek state and one of its founders, who was assassinated on the steps of a church in Nafplion, became a figure in the Greek pantheon similar to Abraham Lincoln in American civil religion.[2]

The church in Greece not only influenced the formation of Greek civil religion but was also profoundly influenced by it. The struggle of the Greek nation for its independence from the Ottoman empire incurred the struggle of the Greek church for its independence—autocephaly—from the Patriarchate of Constantinople. The Greek autocephaly thus became a part

---

2. Yiorgos Lakopoulos, "Lincoln," *Ta Nea*, December 21, 2012, https://tinyurl.com/ybuea9ve.

of the civil religion. Archimandrite Theoklitos Pharmakidis (1784–1860), who played a key role in the proclamation of the Greek autocephaly in 1833, was also a central figure in articulating the doctrine of Greek civil religion.

During the twentieth century, Greek civil religion demonstrated instability and vulnerability to coercive methods. Several times it became a coercive political religion during dictatorships. One such dictatorship was the regime of Ioannis Metaxas, who ruled from 1936 to 1941. Metaxas saw his mission in accomplishing the ideals of the Greek civil religion as they were articulated in the nineteenth century. However, by using violence against his opponents and indoctrinating his subjects, he transformed this civil religion into a political one. In particular, Metaxas believed in the superiority of the state over individuals.[3] His state was totalitarian and in this regard ideologically close to Mussolini's fascist state, with which Metaxas nevertheless had a military clash in 1940. Metaxas also mimicked some structures and ideologemes of the Third Reich.[4] *Mein Kampf* was widely published and read in Metaxas's Greece. The "National Organization of Youth" (Ἐθνική Ὀργάνωσις Νεολαίας) imitated *Hitlerjügend*,[5] and the Greek security services were built on

3. See P.J. Vatikiotis, *Popular Autocracy in Greece, 1936–1941: A Political Biography of General Ioannis Metaxas* (London: Frank Cass, 1998), 185.
4. See Stephen J. Lee, *European Dictatorships 1918–1945* (London: Routledge, 2016), 26.

the model of *SS* and *Gestapo*. Even so, Metaxas's regime should not be completely identified with Nazism. Although it envisaged a pure Greek race taking full control of Greece, it was not anti-Semitic. Metaxas reasonably distanced himself from both Hitler and Mussolini. He was afraid that they would violate the national sovereignty of Greece.

Metaxas died from illness in the beginning of 1941, and the Nazis soon invaded Greece. The occupation continued until 1944, when the German troops decided to withdraw under the pressure from the developments in the eastern front, from the Allies, and from the local *résistance*. The liberation of Greece from Nazis, however, did not bring peace to the country, which became tormented by civil war (1946–1949). It was a war between the Greek troops that participated in the *résistance*, many of them driven by communist ideas and supported by the Soviet Union, and pro-government groups, many of them with roots in the Metaxas regime. After the civil war, which ended with the defeat of the pro-Communist side, the struggle between the political right and left continued.

It led to a strong reappearance of the Greek political religion during a dictatorship that lasted from 1967 to 1974. The so-called "Junta of black colonels" under the leadership of Georgios Papadopoulos (1919–1970) seized political power through a coup d'état. The polit-

5. See John Carr, *The Defence and Fall of Greece: 1940–41* (Barnsley: Pen et Sword Military, 2013), 9.

ical program of the "colonels" featured conservatism and nationalism. Its slogan was "Greece of the Greek Christians" (Ἑλλάς, Ἑλλήνων Χριστιανῶν).[6] In pursuing this political program, the military regime violated the Greek Constitution and proceeded to arrest and murder its political opponents.

A strong conservative and nationalistic agenda blended with references to the Byzantine past encouraged the church in Greece to accept and endorse the Junta. This support came from all ranks and strata within the church. For instance, among the protagonists of the new political regime, there were the lay religious organizations or brotherhoods *Zoi* ("Life") and *Sotir* ("Savior"). The Archbishop of Athens Hieronymos (1905–1988, primate of the Orthodox Church of Greece 1967–1973) in his interview to *Der Spiegel* confessed that "we are very grateful to the army, which saved Greece."[7] A revered spiritual authority, *gerontas* (elder) Theoklitos (1916–2006) from the monastery of St. Dionysios at Mount Athos, notoriously praised one of the Junta's leaders, Stylianos Pattakos (1912–2016), who had mentioned that "we have God as our ally":

6. See G. Karayanni, *Ekklisia ke kratos 1833-1977, istoriki episkopisi ton skheseon tus* [The Church and the State in 1833–1977: A Historical Survey of Their Relations] (Athens: To Pontiki, 1997), 167.

7. W. Fischer, E. Rondholz, and G. Farantu, *Epanastasi ke antepanastasi stin Ellada (1936-1974)* [The Revolution and Counter-Revolution in Greece (1936–1974)] (Athens: Bukumani, 1974), 118. It should be noted here that after August 1969, Hieronymos began warning the regime about excessive use of violence.

We waited for the decades to hear such a language, which expresses the Helleno-Christian Spirit. It is a language of faith, a language both Christian and Greek, which utters the fearless classical bravery of the national soul and the unwavering stability regarding the destinies of the people, which the Orthodox faith in God provides. . . . The high content of this phrase not only sets out a blazing separating line between the vicious and most atheistic past of the recent decades, and the morning of April 21, which brought to our place the Helleno-Christian aura; it also renews memories about the foundations and living experience of our Byzantium. Wherefore our hearts are captivated and our mind is broadened by the idea and hope of a return to the national foundations. . . . The Revolution towards the salvation of the Orthodox Greece from the atheist Communism was a sign from God.[8]

Despite such enthusiastic support from the church, the regime instigated multiple violations against its authority. Soon after seizing political power, the regime replaced the Archbishop of Athens Chrysostomos II (1962–1967) with its own cadre, Archbishop Hieronymos I. Several hierarchs, who did not favor the new regime, were also replaced with more loyal metropolitans. The synod of the church was reshuffled. The common judgment regarding these steps is that they were non-canonical.[9]

8. SMP, "I mavri vivlos tu Elliniku katikhismu" [The Black Book of the Greek Catechetism], *Khristianiki*, March 8, 1974, 6.
9. See Kharis Andreopulos, *I Ekklisia kata ti Diktatoria (1967–1974): istoriki ke*

The Greek church's reputation continued diminishing after the dictatorship was overthrown following the "Polytechnic" rebellion (Πολυτεχνείο [Polytekhneio]). During the process of transition to democracy (Μεταπολίτευσις [Metapolitefsis]), the church was forced out of many public domains of Greek society. The reputation of the church has never been fully restored. Both the short-term and long-term consequences of the collaboration of the Greek Orthodox church with the dictatorship from 1967 to 1974 demonstrate that political religion cannot benefit the church. The church always loses when it supports politically coercive religion for any reason: ideological, political, or financial. The Greek case also provides the general rule about political religions: they tend to challenge the basics of Christianity and deform the structures of the church.

The Romanian Case

The evolution of Romanian civil religion aligns in many regards with its Greek counterpart. Some features from the archetypal Neo-Hellenic civil religion advanced further in Romania, particularly the nationalistic element. The original Neo-Hellenic nationalism was counterbalanced by the Greek universalist past. Romania had no such a counterbalance. As a result,

nomokanoniki prosengisi [The Church and the Dictatorship (1967–1974): A Historical and Canonical Approach] (Thessaloniki: Epikentro, 2017).

its nationalism was more particularist and isolationist. Nationalism is the first and most important article of the Romanian civil religion. Nicolae Iorga (1871–1940), one of the ideologues of this religion, articulated the integral character of Romanian nationalism as follows:

> Nationalism is a doctrine that, once understood, cannot be abandoned, for there are no arguments that can destroy it. There are many who do not imagine that nationalism is also a special way to understand and judge all current problems of our life—political, economic, and cultural—which, given our conditions at this moment—the need to transform all things on the basis of a reality which must be our own and must reflect our own being—is therefore, at the same time, also a moral note.[10]

Just as it did in Greece, civil religion in Romania emerged as an instrument facilitating the transition from the pieces of empires to an independent nation. The pieces from which civil religion helped to stitch a single nation were Wallachia, Moldavia, and Transylvania. They were subjects of the Ottoman, Russian, and Austro-Hungarian empires, respectively. Emancipation began in Transylvania, while Wallachia and Moldavia played a key role in unifying the Romanian

10. Nicolae Iorga, "What Is Nationalism?," in *Eastern European Nationalism in the Twentieth Century*, ed. Peter F. Sugar, trans. James P. Niessen (Lanham, MD: American University Press, 1995), 273–74.

state. The core of this state was composed of the union of Wallachia and Moldavia in 1859.

Like in Greece, the political consolidation of the Romanian lands depended on the construction of a single ethnic identity. This identity was to a significant extent artificial and mythical,[11] as were most national identities that emerged in the nineteenth century. This identity was constructed on the basis of some events from the past that were eclectically stitched together to give the new nation a feeling of its rootedness in history. The goal of such mythical constructions is always to make a nation perceive its identity as perennial, almost eternal. In the Romanian case, its past, constructed in the frame of civil religion, was more legendary than in the Greek case.

A key element of the Romanian primordial past was a myth of two Roman legions that participated in the military campaign in Dacia around 110 CE. Soldiers from those legions reportedly took wives from among local women. The Romanian people thus came from intermarriages between Romans and Dacians. This story cannot be confirmed by historical evidence. Nevertheless, it constitutes the legendary core of the Romanian civil religion—its "myth of origin."[12] Called the theory of "Daco-Roman Romanian community," it

11. See Geoffrey Hosking and George Schöpflin, eds., *Myths and Nationhood* (London: Hurst, 1997).
12. See Robert Bellah, *The Broken Covenant: American Civil Religion in Time of Trial* (Chicago: University of Chicago Press, 1992), 4.

was constructed by Romanian intellectuals in the nineteenth century. The Romanian Orthodox church also actively contributed to the legend and integrated it to the "vita" of the nation, as it were. According to this pious "vita," the Roman soldiers were Christians. While Greek civil religion referred to the Holy Trinity in order to support the idea of three historical stages of the same nation, Romanian civil religion built on the story of allegedly Christian Romans and heathen Dacians uniting in the single Romanian nation in a similar manner to the two natures in Jesus Christ.

There are two modern ecclesial figures who can be considered protagonists of the Romanian civil religion: the Greek Catholic bishop Inocenţiu Micu-Klein (1692–1768) and the Orthodox Metropolitan of Sibiu Andrei Şaguna (1809–1873). Inocenţiu was behind the petitions for recognition of the Romanian nation presented in 1791 to the Habsburgs. They are known as *Supplex Libellus Valachorum* and constitute a "birth certificate of the Romanian nation."[13] As Cristian Romocea remarks, "Bishop Inocenţiu remains a symbol of national emancipation. The real contribution to the identification between Romanian nationalism and Orthodoxy was made by Şaguna."[14] The two hierarchs thus represent two different stages of the Romanian

---

13. Angelika Schaser, *Reformele iosefine în Transilvania şi urmările lor în viaţa socială* [The Josephine Reforms in Transylvania and Their Consequences in Social Life] (Sibiu: Hora, 2000), 214.

14. Cristian Romocea, *Church and State: Religious Nationalism and State Identification in Post-Communist Romania* (London: Continuum, 2011), 118.

civil religion: one of emancipation and the other of nation-building.

Alexandru Ioan Cuza, the ruler (*Domnitor*) of the Romanian principalities (1859–1866), orchestrated forging different legendary and historical elements into a sacred narrative that shaped the Romanian national identity. Cuza managed to unify the Romanian principalities in 1859 and can be regarded an architect of Romanian civil religion. He also led the battle for independence—autocephaly—of the Romanian church from the Patriarchate of Constantinople. The Romanian autocephaly, similarly to the earlier Greek autocephaly, became a part of the civil religion program. The unification of autonomous Romanian churches followed and thus sacralized the unification of the Romanian lands. The two Romanian metropolitanates, in Bucharest (Wallachia) and Iaşi (Moldavia), were united in 1865 under the common leadership of one Romanian primate in Bucharest. This church was then proclaimed autocephalous six years after the political unification of Wallachia and Moldavia. The Romanian autocephaly was not recognized for twenty years, until it was eventually accepted by Constantinople in 1885.

Like in Greece, autocephaly as a means of incorporating the church into civil religion meant more control and interference of the state in the matters of the church. Cuza created mechanisms for state control over the church similar to the mechanisms that had been created earlier in Greece. He put bishops under his control through the primate of the church, took finances of the church into his own hands and secularized church lands. Those who disagreed with him, such as Metropolitan Sofronie Miclescu of Moldavia (1790–1861), were deposed through the synod that he orchestrated.[15]

Most political figures in Romania continued building the local civil religion. One of them, Nicolae Iorga, made his contribution in several capacities: as a publicist and public speaker, a prime-minister (in the years 1931–32), and a scholar in the field of Byzantine studies. His book *Byzance après Byzance*[16] became a classic on the survival of Byzantine civilization after the fall of the Byzantine empire. As a politician, he envisaged the modern Romanian state as a "Byzantium after Byzantium."[17] He made the Byzantine past an intrinsic part of Romanian civil religion. However, just like in Greece, fascination about Byzantium was among the factors that instigated the transformation of civil religion into coercive political religion.

In Romania, violent political religion gradually replaced civil religion in the 1930s and lasted for almost the rest of the century, until the regime of Nico-

---

15. See Lucian N. Leustean, ed., *Orthodox Christianity and Nationalism in Nineteenth-Century Southeastern Europe* (New York: Fordham University Press, 2014), 117.

16. Nicolae Iorga, *Byzance après Byzance: continuation de l'histoire de la vie byzantine* [Byzantium after Byzantium: The Continuation of the History of Byzantine Life] (Bucarest: L'Institut d'études byzantines, 1935).

17. See Romocea, *Church and State*, 77.

lae Ceauşescu was overthrown in 1989. It had two opposing phases: one was pro-monarchy, pro-church, and anti-communist, and the other was communist and anti-church. Despite all of their differences, these phases of Romanian political religion were similar in authoritarian methods and religious zeal in achieving their goals. As well, they were perpetrated, to a larger or lesser extent, by the church.[18]

The earliest phase of Romanian political religion began with the establishment of the right-wing nationalist "Legion of Archangel Michael" (*Legiunea Arhanghelului Mihail*) in 1927. Its founder was Corneliu Zelea Codreanu (1899–1938), referred to as "The Capitan" (*Căpitanul*). In 1930, the paramilitary branch of the movement was called "Iron Guard" (*Garda de Fier*), which eventually gave its name to the entire movement. In the 1930s, the movement became a political party that won seats in the Parliament.

The "Legion" embraced most elements of the extant civil religion. Its self-identification, "Legion," was a reference to the Roman legions in Dacia and thus endorsed the theory of "Daco-Roman Romanian community." The allusion to the archangel Michael signified a strong adherence to the Orthodox church. Indeed, among the main goals of the "Legion" was the promotion of Romanian nationalism *and* religion. Its program stated that it was "an organization based on

18. See Lucian N. Leustean, *Orthodoxy and the Cold War* (New York: Palgrave Macmillan, 2009).

order and discipline, guided by a pure nationalism, protecting the altars of the church, which its enemies wish to dismantle."[19] Mircea Eliade (1907–1986), a famous scholar of religion at the University of Chicago, in his young years supported the "Legion" and served as its ideologue. He then stressed the religious agenda of the movement:

> The Legionary movement has a spiritual and Christian meaning. If all the contemporary revolutions have as their goal the conquest of power by a social class or by a man, the Legionary solution aims, on the contrary, at the supreme redemption of the nation, the reconciliation of the Romanian nation with God, as the Captain [Cordeanu] said. That is why the Legionary movement has a different meaning with regard to everything that has been done up till now in history; and the victory of the Legion will lead not only to the restoration of the virtues of our nation, of a hardworking Romania, worthy and powerful, but also to the birth of a man who is in harmony with the new kind of European life.[20]

As the "legionnaires" pledged to support the church, so they expected the church to support the "Legion." The church did not fail to meet their expectations. As Romanian priest Fr. Ilie Imbrescu (1909–1949) wrote in

---

19. In Romocea, *Church and State*, 136.
20. Mircea Eliade, *Buna Vestire* [Good News], January 14, 1938, quoted in Radu Ioanid, "The Sacralised Politics of the Romanian Iron Guard," in *Fascism, Totalitarianism and Political Religion*, ed. Roger Griffin (London: Routledge, 2005), 143.

his 1940 book *The Church and the Legionary Movement*, "A true priest will therefore be a Legionnaire by the nature of things, just as a Legionnaire will be in his turn, and again by the nature of things, a Legionnaire, the best son of the Church."[21] The church blended with the "Legion." For example, in Parliament, after the elections in 1937, 33 out of 103 representatives of the Iron Guard Party were Orthodox priests. The "Legion" was particularly popular among the Romanian clergy and laity. At the same time, a significant number of bishops were not happy about its program and activities, which challenged their own authority in the church. For instance, the first Romanian Patriarch Miron Cristea (1868–1939) tried to restrict the Guard's influence upon the church. He was particularly successful in his policies against the Guard, when in February 1938 he was appointed prime minister of Romania by King Carol II. Carol had just dismissed the elected parliament and government, and established dictatorship. Patriarch Miron, by accepting the position of prime minister, was instrumental in increasing the legitimacy of the king's dictatorship.

The dictatorship of Carol did not last for long and was soon replaced by another dictatorship. This one was formed by the alliance of the "Legion" and the general Ion Antonescu (1882–1946). Through their collaboration, they established a state, which was called

21. Ilie Imbrescu, *Biserica şi Mişcarea Legionară* [The Church and the Legionary Movement] (Bucharest: Cartea Românească, 1940), 201.

"National Legionary State" (*Statul Național Legionar*, from September 6, 1940 to January 23, 1941). It was a one-party state, with the "Legion" as its only legal political party. Antonescu was granted honorary leadership in the "Legion," while the leader of the "Legion" at that time, Horia Sima (1906–1993), became deputy premier of the government. Soon, however, the "Legion" and Antonescu clashed in a conflict, from which Antonescu came out victorious. Nazi Germany played an important role in the conflict. Some of its leaders, such as Joseph Goebbels, supported the "Legion." Hitler, however, extended more help to Antonescu. At the same time, he granted Horia Sima political asylum after he had been sentenced to death by the Romanian dictator.

The Romanian church enthusiastically supported Antonescu after his victory. Patriarch Nicodim Munteanu (1864–1948), who recently compared the king Carol II with the Roman emperor Constantine, now became a passionate supporter of Carol's enemy, Antonescu. In one of his speeches Nicodim stated characteristically, "God had shown to the leader of our country [Antonescu] the path toward a sacred and redeeming alliance with the German nation and sent the united armies to the Divine Crusade against the destructive Bolshevism."[22]

Not just Nicodim, but most far-right and pro-church

22. In Romocea, *Church and State*, 135.

political groups and figures in Romania before and during World War II expressed sympathy with Nazism. Many of them developed their own version of fascist ideology. Radu Ioanid identified the following features of Romanian fascism as common to all groups: "Nationalism, antisemitism and racism, the cult of the supreme leader and of its own élite, mysticism, the social diversion, and finally anticommunism."[23]

The difference between Romanian fascism and its German or Italian counterparts lay in its strong support of the official church. According to Cristian Romocea, "The Iron Guard became the only European Fascist movement with religion at its core."[24] Romanian fascism was also the most metaphysical movement among its peers. I. P. Prundeni, a legionnaire journalist, published in 1937 an essay titled "God Is Fascist" (*Dumnezu e fascist*).[25] The approach of the Romanian fascists to their nation was similar to the Nazi approach to the Aryan race. Romanians envisaged a pure Romanian race distilled by eugenics.[26] A prominent Romanian eugenicist, racial scientist, and ideologue of the "Legion," Traian Herseni (1907–1980), stated in this regard:

23. Ioanid, "Sacralised Politics," 125.
24. Romocea, *Church and State,* 134.
25. I. P. Prundeni, "Dumnezu e fascist" [God is Fascist], *Porunca Vremii,* July 20, 1937.
26. See Vladimir Solonari, *Purifying the Nation: Population Exchange and Ethnic Cleansing in Nazi-Allied Romania* (Baltimore: Johns Hopkins University Press, 2010).

The racial purification of the Romanian people is a question of life and death. There are several ways to solve this problem. To begin with, it must be precisely determined as to the racial characteristics to which the Romanian people owe their present-day creations and their periods of historical flowering, as well as their moral and political defeats, their periods of decadence and of historical shame. . . . We must struggle against everything that is foreign to our nation and against everything that constitutes a baneful influence, and encourage, in exchange, everything that is authentically Romanian.[27]

Thus, the initial romantic nationalism, which was a feature of Romanian civil religion during the nineteenth century, in the 1930s turned into a sort of racism that placed other nations below the Romanians. At the top of the hierarchy of nations in Romania was Dacian identity. Even the Roman or Latin identities were inferior to it. Below the Romanians, there were other nations, even if they were Orthodox, such as Greeks or Ukrainians. Jews were at the very bottom of this hierarchy.

The Russian Case

Both Russian civil and political religion differ from the two previous cases. Unlike the Balkan iterations, which

27. Traian Herseni, "Rasa si destin national" [Race and National Destiny], *Cuvîntul*, January 16, 1941.

were more particularist and focused on the formation and preservation of a *nation*, the Russian version is more universalist and focused on sustaining the *empire*. The Russian civil and political religions are thus imperial and imperialist, respectively.

These religions developed in three phases. The first one was tsarist; the second one, Soviet; and the third, post-Soviet. These phases evolved as a dialectical process: the tsarist phase set the thesis, the Soviet phase was its antithesis, and the final phase synthesized elements from both preceding phases. While it is relatively easy to draw a clear line of demarcation between civil and political religions in other cases, it is much harder to do so in Russia's case. In Russia, civil religions always featured elements of violent political religion, and vice versa. In other words, the Russian civil/political religion was violent all the time—sometimes more and sometimes less.

The roots of this religion go back to early modernity, into which the archaic Russian society was forcefully initiated by Peter I Romanov "the Great" (1672–1725). He was the architect of this religion, which he violently imposed on his subjects and on the Russian church. The church tried to resist but eventually yielded to the will of the tsar and endorsed his religion.

One of the earliest manifestations of this religion was the anathema against the Ukrainian het'man Ivan Mazepa (1639–1709). Mazepa, as a semi-autonomous ruler of the Ukrainians, was an ally of Peter in the

Great Northern War (1700–1721), where Russia fought against Poland and Sweden. The Ukrainian het'man was dissatisfied with the centralization of Peter's power, which threatened the autonomy of the Ukrainians protected by the Treaty of Pereyaslav (1654). As a result, he decided to change sides in the war and allied himself with the king of Sweden, Charles XII (1682–1718).

Mazepa's switch infuriated Peter. As revenge for Mazepa's actions, which he viewed as a betrayal, Peter pillaged the capital of the Ukrainian autonomy Baturyn, killing the cossack garrison there and many of its civil inhabitants. He ordered the bodies of dead cossacks to be tied to crosses and floated down the Dnieper River. This was a symbolic act intended to imitate Mazepa's flight down the same river to Moldavia. Peter proceeded to commit another symbolic act and ordered the church hierarchs to anathematize Mazepa. Initially done by the Ukrainian bishops, the anathema was later confirmed by the Russian hierarchs. Mazepa's name was included in the list of the traitors who were publicly anathematized in all Russian churches during the Feast of Orthodoxy. The *History of Rusy* describes the original anathema:

> The priests and monks, who were brought from all corners, were vested in black and held in their hands long candles smeared with soot. While singing hymns, they surrounded the effigy. Then, while turning black candles to the effigy, they shouted with deacons and sex-

tons: "Let be Mazepa cursed." Then the bishop struck the breast of the effigy with a stick and shouted: "To the apostate and traitor Mazepa—anathema." Then the effigy was dragged from the church, followed by the clergy who sang: "Now Judas abandons the disciple and receives the devil."[28]

What looked like a "black mass" was in effect a ritual of the new coercive political religion. The church was forcefully drawn by Peter to participate in it. Soon coercion was applied to the church itself. The same year (1721), when Peter proclaimed himself an "emperor," he reorganized the Russian church according to his own preferences. The tsar promulgated a "Spiritual Regulation," which replaced the patriarchal office with the "Most Holy Governing Synod." This replacement turned the Russian church from a partner of the state, in some periods as powerful as the state itself, as in the time of the patriarch Nikon (1605–1658), into a piece of the repressive state machinery. The leadership of the church, which was placed under the control of the state through the office of the "Ober-prokuror" of the Synod, effectively became a part of the state bureaucracy. Together with other newly established ministries, the Synod was expected to implement the political will of the emperor. The church was thus subsumed by the state and assigned a

28. George Konisky, *Istoriya Rusov ili Maloy Rosii. Sochineniye Georgiya Koniskago, Arkhiepiskopa Beloruskago* [*The History of Rusy or Small Russia. A Work by George Konisky, the Archbishop of Belarus'*] (Moscow: University Press, 1846), 212.

formal political role. Among the goals of this political role was to legitimize the imperial authority and its political actions.

The Russian political religion was conceived by the tsar but delivered by the church figures, such as the Archbishop of Novgorod Feofan Prokopovich (1681–1736), who penned the *Spiritual Regulation*. Feofan was a designer of the new mechanism of church-state relations in the Russian empire, which gave all power over the church to the head of the state. In its coercive form, this religion lasted almost the entire eighteenth century, which witnessed a forceful secularization of church lands and persecutions against those hierarchs who disagreed with the imperial policies towards the church, such as the Metropolitan of Rostov Arseniy Matseyevytch (1697–1772) and the Metropolitan of Tobol'sk Pavel Konyuskevych (1705–1770).

The political religion of the Russian empire became less coercive and more civilized in the beginning of the nineteenth century, during the reign of Alexander I (reigned 1801–1825). His reign was the birth period of civil religion in Russia, which, unlike in most other cases, emerged not prior to but after the political religion. The Russian civil religion sprang from the Russian war with Napoleon—the so-called "Patriotic War" of 1812. Leo Tolstoy (1828–1910), in his novel *War and Peace*, captured the moment of its birth and identified its features: patriotism, monarchism, and faithfulness to the traditions and religion of the Russian past. The Cathedral of Christ the Savior in Moscow, built to commemorate the Russian victories and losses in the Napoleonic wars, became the national shrine of civil religion. Under the conservative Nikolai I (reigned 1825–1855), Russian civil religion began worshiping three "hypostases" of the Russian empire: Orthodoxy, monarchy, and peopleness (Православие-самодержавие-народность). This trinitarian formula, coined by the Russian official Sergey Uvarov (1786–1855), became the credo of Russian civil religion. Its reference to the Trinity was similar to the formula of Greek civil religion, articulated in approximately the same period by Konstantinos Paparrigopoulos.

Ideas that fed Russian civil religion developed further within the framework of the Slavophile movement. This movement believed in a unique historical destiny for and the originality (самобытность) of the Russian people. Slavophiles were inspired by Romanticism, which was fashionable in the early nineteenth century, and borrowed many ideas from German idealistic philosophy. The movement was founded by Aleksey Khomyakov (1804–1860), Ivan Kireyevskiy (1806–1856), brothers Konstantin (1817–1860) and Ivan Asksakov (1823–1886), and Yuriy Samarin (1819–1876).

The most insightful prophet of the Russian civil religion was Fyodor Dostoevsky (1821–1881). One of the characters in his novel *The Devils* (1872) is Ivan Shatov, a former atheist who converts to civil religion. Shatov effectively articulates the creed of this religion: "I believe in Russia. I believe in the Greek Orthodox Church. I—I believe in the body of Christ—I believe that the second coming will take place in Russia." When asked a clarifying question—"But in God? In God?"—Shatov replies, "I—I shall believe in God."[29] As Shatov articulates, Russian civil religion has required belief in the historic mission of Russia, but not necessarily belief in God.

As mentioned earlier, Russian civil religion was never completely free of coercion and therefore never quite civil. The Russian state enforced the credo "Orthodoxy, monarchy, and peopleness," and those who thought differently were persecuted. Dostoyevsky in his early years was among those who thought differently. He participated in the anti-government political activities and was sentenced to execution. His execution, however, was in the last moment replaced by exile to Siberia, where he spent four years. This experience of dying and then coming back to life changed his worldview radically. It became religious and patriotic, and turned him from a victim to an advocate of the civil religion. He articulated it in more detail in his diaries and other public writings. In particular, Dostoevsky wrote about the "Russian Christ" and "Russian

29. Fyodor Dostoyevsky, *The Devils*, trans. David Magarshack (New York: Penguin, 1971), 259.

God,"[30] who became the main "deity" of Russian civil religion.

Although Dostoevsky envisaged Russian civil religion as nonviolent, he could not control the religion he professed. It soon reversed back to its earlier coercive forms. The coercive nature of the religion was particularly marked by pogroms, which became common on the eve of the Russian revolutions in the beginning of the twentieth century. Pogroms were rituals of the Russian imperial political religion. Grigoriy Rasputin (1869–1916)—an "elder" who exercised unlimited influence on the family of the last Russian tsar Nikolai II Romanov (1868–1918, reigned 1894–1917)—became the icon of this imperial religion.

The imperial political religion was upheld until the first Russian revolution in February 1917, when the monarchy was replaced by a short-lived republican democracy, which was in turn replaced by dictatorship, when the Bolsheviks seized power in October 1917. In the period between February and October, there was no official civil or political religion in Russia. This period provided the Russian Orthodox Church with unprecedented opportunities for revival without being distracted by political agendas. The church restored the office of patriarch, which had been abolished by Peter I, and convened its great council, which

---

30. From the letter to A. N. Maikov on December 11 (23), 1868, in F. M. Dostoevsky, *Sobraniye sochineniy v 15 tomakh* [Collection of Works in 15 Volumes] (St. Petersburg: Nauka, 1996), 15:390.

had been impeded by Nikolai II. This council adopted a program of *aggiornamento*, which was halted by the return of a new edition of the Russian political religion.

After the Bolshevik revolution in October 1917, the Russian state endorsed an extremely violent political religion. Atheism effectively became an established religion of the Soviet state. This religion had its own rites and dogmas. Its Moses and Aaron were Karl Marx and Friedrich Engels, and its messiah was Vladimir Lenin, whose relics were venerated in the Mausoleum and icons kept in every house and office. Marxism-Leninism constituted its Orthodoxy, while Trotskyism, Maoism, Titoism, and the like were its heresies. The Communist Party as the magisterium decided what was Orthodoxy and what was heresy. The Party interpreted the doctrine at its ecumenical councils—the Congresses.

The Soviet political regime was fundamentally coercive. Its coercive nature peaked during Iosif Stalin's tenure as the Soviet leader (from 1929 to 1953). Stalin created a gigantic infrastructure of violence and killing. Holodomor—massive famine in the early 1930s—and Gulag—a system of concentration camps, where most people perished in the late 1930s—became the symbols of this coercive religion. Rudolf Rummel, who studied the democides of the twentieth century, estimates that Stalin murdered around 62 million of his co-citizens.[31]

After the collapse of communism in the early 1990s,

all forms of civil and political religion were abandoned by the state—much like the period following the democratic revolution in February 1917. The church was set free from persecution and oppression. There was powerful momentum for a spiritual renaissance in Russia. This period, however, did not last long, and soon the Orthodox renaissance turned to the renaissance of political Orthodoxy: "post-Soviet civil religion."[32]

This religion began not with the state but the church. To reoccupy the public space from which it had been expelled in the Soviet period, and to facilitate its mission in post-communist society, the Russian Orthodox Church sought to fill the void left by communist propaganda. Its initial intention was to replace communist ideology with Christianity. In reality, however, a new ideology under the guise of Christianity substituted the old communist doctrine.

Post-Soviet civil religion is eclectic and has included elements from the pre-Soviet and Soviet periods. From the former, it has borrowed the idea of the originality (самобытность) of the Russian people and such figures as Tsar Nikolai II. From the latter, it has adopted ethical values embedded in the "Moral Code of the Builder of Communism." The eclectic character of post-Soviet

31. Rudolph Joseph Rummel, *Death by Government* (New Brunswick: Transaction, 2008), 79.
32. Sergey Chapnin first identified this phenomenon in *Tserkov' v postsovietskoy Rossii. Vozrozhdeniye, kachestvo very, dialog s obschestvom* [The Church in Post-Soviet Russia: Revival, Quality of Faith, Dialogue with Society] (Moscow: Arefa, 2013).

civil religion is best manifested in the cult of the Patriotic War. As mentioned earlier, the Patriotic War of 1812 against Napoleon was the founding event for pre-Soviet civil religion. In the Soviet era, The Great Patriotic War of 1941–1945 against Hitler substituted it. Leonid Brezhnev (leader of the Soviet state from 1964 to 1982) designated it as a "sacred war" and made it a core of Soviet civil religion. In post-Soviet civil religion, both patriotic wars conflated into the single cult of victory against the West celebrated widely with religious zeal.

The articles of faith of the new civil religion in Russia have been articulated on the platform of the so-called "World Russian People's Council" (Всемирный русский народный собор). This council also reflects the eclectic character of post-Soviet civil religion. On the one hand, it refers to the ideas of "conciliarity" (соборность) articulated by Aleksey Khomyakov and thus can be seen as a continuation of pre-Soviet civil religion. On the other hand, it resembles the Congresses of the Communist Party in the Soviet period—the chief forum of Soviet political religion.

The political leadership of modern Russia was initially hesitant to employ the rhetoric and dogmas of post-Soviet civil religion developed within the Russian church and on the margins of Russian society. However, during his third term as president of the Russian Federation (2012–2018), Vladimir Putin eventually adopted it as a new ideology of the Russian state.

After becoming a state religion, civil religion turned into a political religion. The turning point was the trial of the punk group Pussy Riot for its performance in the Orthodox cathedrals in Moscow in February 2012. The performance, called "Mother of God, Drive Putin Away," infuriated the president of the Russian Federation. The Russian Orthodox Church initiated legal prosecution of the members of the group, who were eventually sentenced to two years behind bars. After this episode, the coercive post-Soviet political religion developed rapidly.

This religion rearranged its pantheon. Softer civil saints, such as Tsar Nikolai II, were replaced by harder ones, such as Iosif Stalin and Tsar Ivan the Terrible (1530–1584). Alexandr Dugin (born in 1962), a faithful member of the Russian Orthodox Church, is a key ideologue of this religion. His doctrine of "Eurasianism" envisages an original (самобытная) Eurasian civilization different from liberal Western civilization. Dugin sees Byzantium as a model for such civilization. He explains Byzantium as an eternal principle, or *archē*, of the Russian historical mission. Byzantium, for Dugin, is not only about the past but also about the present and the future of Russia. Dugin preaches Byzantium as an absolute value along with the absolute value of God and of the church. For Dugin, Byzantium was a chiliastic kingdom of Jesus Christ. In this kingdom, the devil was bound, and his epigone, the antichrist, was kept away by the emperor, whom Dugin presents as the biblical "katechon" (2 Thess 2:6–7).[33] Notably, Carl Schmitt (1888–1985), an ideologue of the Third Reich, also made references to "katechon."[34]

As with other totalitarian ideologies that emerged in Orthodox contexts, references to Byzantium join Dugin's call for violence. Indeed, he has repeatedly called for the use of violence to fulfil the Byzantine mission of Russian civilization. In a video statement, he urged the Russians to "kill, kill, and kill" the Ukrainians who dared to revolt against being included in the geopolitical sphere of the neo-Soviet empire.[35] Thus, the violent post-Soviet political religion, which began with the Pussy Riot episode, culminated in the Russian aggression against Ukraine that followed the Ukrainian Revolution of Dignity during the winter of 2013–2014. Russia launched this war to prevent the process of democratization, which had been instigated by the protests against the corrupted and violent authorities at the Maidan in Kyiv, from spreading to Russia. Russian propaganda presented the annexation of Crimea and intrusion to the east of Ukraine as a holy

---

33. "Aleksander Dugin: Vizantiya—nashe vechnoye nachalo" [Byzantium—our Eternal Principle], YouTube video, 18:19, uploaded by Tsar'grad TV, November 26, 2015, https://tinyurl.com/y99nzt8n.

34. Carl Schmitt, *The Nomos of the Earth in the International Law of the Jus Publicum Europaeum*, trans. G. L. Ulmen (New York: Telos, 2006), 59–60. See Julia Hell, "Katechon: Carl Schmitt's Imperial Theology and the Ruins of the Future," *The Germanic Review: Literature, Culture, Theory* 84, no. 4 (2009): 283–326.

35. "Aleksander Dugin: Ubivat', ubivat' ubivat'" [Alexander Dugin: To Kill, Kill, and Kill], YouTube video, 2:50, uploaded by "Randy Mandy," June 15, 2014, https://tinyurl.com/y7o2ncwj.

war of Russian Orthodox civilization against the presumably godless West. Thousands of Russian mercenaries, together with local collaborators, led by Russian officers and supplied with Russian weapons, were mobilized by the doctrine of the "Russian world."

The roots of this doctrine go back to the nineteenth century, when the Slavophiles developed Panslavism—a doctrine of unity of the Slavic nations under the leadership of Russia. It reemerged on the Russian political scene soon after the collapse of the Soviet Union. Its initial version was relatively peaceful. It aimed at consolidation of the Russian-speaking people outside of Russia as an instrument of soft power. After the victory of the Ukrainian Maidan, however, it turned into an engine of war. The Russian Orthodox Church first made the "Russian world" a civil religion and later contributed to its transformation into a violent political religion. The "Russian world" became a personal project of the Patriarch of Moscow Kirill (in office since 2009), and a new stage in the evolution of Russian civil/political religions. Indeed, the church, in contrast to earlier Soviet and pre-Soviet versions of civil/political religions produced by the state, took a lead in constructing their post-Soviet version. While the church played a secondary role in earlier versions of civil/political religions in Russia, in post-Soviet Russia, its role is primary.

As mentioned earlier, Orthodox hierarchs corroborated Tsar Peter's political religion in the early eighteenth century. The church stood by the tsarist state during the nineteenth century and blessed the transformation of its civil religion to the violent religion of pogroms. After the collapse of the Russian empire, the Russian hierarchs continued collaborating with all political religions of the twentieth century inside and outside Russia. Because these political religions were antagonistic (Nazism versus communism), such collaboration led to schisms within the Russian church. Part of the church, now known as the Russian Orthodox Church Outside Russia (ROCOR), did not accept the Soviet regime. It actively participated in the struggle of the Russian "White" emigration against the Bolsheviks, which eventually led to appeasing Nazism, as illustrated by the greeting letter of the primate of the ROCOR, Metropolitan Anastasiy Gribanovskiy (1873– 1965), to Adolf Hitler:

> Not only the German nation commemorates you with fervent love and devotion to the Throne of the Highest: the best people of all nations, who wish you peace and justice, see you as a leader in the world struggle for peace and truth. . . . Your feat for the German people and the greatness of the German Empire made you an exemplary model worthy of imitation, and a model of how one should love one's people and one's country, how one should stand for national treasures and eternal values. . . . God may strengthen you and the German people in the fight against hostile forces, who wish death to our people. May He give you, your country, your Gov-

ernment and the army good health, prosperity and all the good haste for many years.[36]

As for the Russian Orthodox Church in the Soviet Union, only a part of it did not affiliate itself with any political religion, either tsarist or Soviet. The Patriarch of Moscow Tikhon Belavin (1865–1925), who led this faction of the church, chose to live without any political or civil religion. The price for this choice was high, and Tikhon was put under arrest and died from hardships imposed by the Soviet regime. Many so-called "new martyrs" who perished in the Gulags had made the same choice.

However, Tikhon's successor, Sergiy Stragorodskiy (1867–1944), made a different choice. In 1927, he signed a Declaration of Loyalty to the Soviet regime and its violent political religion. The Declaration stated:

> We, the church leaders, are not together with the enemies of our Soviet state . . . but with our people and our government. . . . We need to show, not in words but in deeds, that not only those who are indifferent to Orthodoxy, not only its renegades can be faithful citizens of the Soviet Union, loyal to the Soviet government, but also the most zealous adherents of Orthodoxy. . . . We want to be Orthodox and at the same time do recognize the Soviet Union as our civic homeland, the joys

---

36. Published in the periodical "*Tserkovnaya zhizn*'" [Church Life] 5, no. 6 (1938): 96.

and successes of which are our joys and successes, and whose failures are our failures.[37]

This document attacked the ROCOR, which allegedly harbored the "enemies of the Soviet state" and became an "insane instrument" of "their intrigues." For the ROCOR, however, the "Soviet church" turned to a "hostile force," which was referred to in Anastasiy's letter to Hitler.

The so-called "Renovationist" (Обновленческая) or "Alive" (Живая) church seemed even more collaborative with the Soviet regime. This church was promoted by the communist regime as a more loyal alternative to the "Patriarchal" church led by Tikhon Belavin. The "Renovationist" church evolved alongside the structures of the Russian Orthodox Church from 1922 to 1936. It embraced some elements of communist ideology. For example, one of its leaders, Fr. Vladimir Krasnitskiy (1881–1936), suggested that this church adopted an oxymoronic doctrine of "materialist Christianity."

Many priests and bishops who chose to collaborate with the oppressive political religions in the twentieth centuries had been proponents of collaboration with the tsarist regime. For instance, both the founder of the ROCOR, Antoniy Khrapovitskiy, and the first Soviet Patriarch Sergiy Stragorodskiy, who would find them-

---

37. First published in the Soviet newspaper *Izvestia* on August 18, 1927. Available at https://tinyurl.com/ycm6wv88.

selves on the opposite sides of the ideological divide, were zealous monarchists prior to 1917. Some leaders of the "Renovationist" church had actively participated in the Black Hundred movement. Father Vladimir Krasnitskiy, for example, who after the Bolshevik revolution promoted "materialist Christianity," before the revolution publicly lectured on the Christian sacrifices allegedly performed by Jews. He also used to be a member of the Black Hundred. Other members of this organization, such as Fr. Tikhon Popov, became active collaborators with the communist regime after the Bolshevik revolution.[38] Their collaboration with oppressive regimes did not change, even when the regimes changed.

As for post-Soviet political religion, as mentioned earlier, the Russian Orthodox Church not only chose to endorse it but also has played a leading role in its formation. The church gave this religion language and symbols. Moreover, it persuaded the state that it needs such a religion. Thus, hierarchs and official speakers of the church contributed to the ethos of coercion, which has dominated Vladimir Putin's Russia. A bestselling book by bishop Tikhon Shevkunov, *Everyday Saints*,[39]

38. M. Agurskiy, *Ideologiya natsional-bolshevizma* [The Ideology of the National Bolshevism] (Paris: YMCA-Press, 1980), 109–10. On Tikhon Popov see V. V. Bureha, "Popov Tykhon Dmytrovych," in *Kyivs'ka dukhovna akademiya v imenakh: 1819–1924* [Kyiv Theological Academy through Names: 1819–1924], ed. M. L. Tkachuk (Kyiv: Kyiv-Mohyla Academy Press, 2016), 2:452–54.

39. Tikhon Shevkunov, *Everyday Saints and Other Stories*, trans. Julian Henry Lowenfeld (Moscow: Pokrov, 2012).

interprets coercion as a form of traditional Orthodox spirituality. Father Vsevolod Chaplin, an official speaker of the church until December 2015, repeatedly endorsed the "anti-Western" war in Ukraine and the "sacred" war in Syria.[40] There is also no lack of praise from the church hierarchs for Mr. Putin, who enforces post-Soviet political religion. The Metropolitan of Odessa Agafangel Savvin (born 1938), for instance, congratulated Mr. Putin for his third term as the president of the Russian Federation. This sample of servile rhetoric is worth quoting in its full length:

> Esteemed Mr. President! On behalf of the clergy and faithful of the Odessa metropolia of the Ukrainian Orthodox Church of the Moscow Patriarchate, of the Orthodox community of Odessa and myself, I cordially congratulate you on a brilliant and blessed by God Victory in the elections of the President of the Russian Federation. We rejoice in your joy. Our prayers are heard by God and accepted by Him. On the March 4, the day of triumph of Orthodoxy the truth of God triumphed, in which "mercy and truth are met, righteousness and peace have kissed each other" (Ps 84:11). Through you, Vladimir Vladimirovich, the healthy forces of the Russian society won, your political opponents and enemies of Russia were decisively rebuked. . . . Merciful Lord,

---

40. See "Eks-spiker RPTs: Luchshe yadernaya voyna, chem Donbass v sostave Ukrainy" [Ex-Speaker of the Russian Orthodox Church: Nuclear War Is Better Than Donbass as Part of Ukraine], *Religion in Ukraine*, May 27, 2016, https://tinyurl.com/yd7moykw; and Fred Weir, "Is Russia's Intervention in Syria a 'Holy War'? Russian Orthodox Church: 'Yes,'" *The Christian Science Monitor*, November 23, 2015, https://tinyurl.com/ybcmebhw.

who cares about salvation of Great Russia, again elected and installed you to the high and responsible position, so that light of your wisdom, charm and warmth of your heart strengthened the thorny path of development of the Russian state at this fateful historical stage. . . . We deeply believe that at this difficult stage of its history the people of Great Russia will once again unite around you as its national leader, highly esteemed Vladimir Vladimirovich, in the name of the Russian statehood and in the name of saving a strong, powerful Russia. I sincerely wish you, the President of the new democratic Russia, an outstanding political and public figure of the Russian state, the faithful son of the Russian people, a citizen and a patriot of the Russian land, health, joy, happiness, inspiration and all-powerful God's help in your upcoming multifaceted creative activities for good of Russia and for prosperity of the Russian state, in celebration of the victory of truth over falsehood, good over evil, in maintaining peace and harmony in the society. This was our fervent prayer. May the heavenly powers keep you! Sincerely, Agafangel, Metropolitan of Odessa and Izmail, honorary citizen of Odessa and the Odessa region, member of the Odessa Regional Council.[41]

The Russian Orthodox Church, through its alignment with the state, thus remains consistent with earlier versions of Russian political religion even though the Tsarist and Soviet versions are incompatible with each other. For example, the church continues to extend

---

41. The Odessa Diocese of the Ukrainian Orthodox Church, accessed April 23, 2018, https://tinyurl.com/ybg74slw.

its support to the anathema of Peter I against Ivan Mazepa and has not condemned the pogroms. Some of its officials even support Grigoriy Rasputin.[42] The church continues to deny the Holodomor, one of the most outrageous crimes of the Stalinist political religion. It increasingly accepts the rehabilitation of Stalin, who almost exterminated the church itself. In 2016, a monument to Stalin was installed in the city of Orel. This action was endorsed by Patriarch Kirill and blessed by his confessor, *starets* (elder) Iliy Nozdrin (born 1932). Finally, the Russian Orthodox Church made possible the Russian aggression against Ukraine through the device of the "Russian world." It has become an intrinsic part of the Russian hybrid war against Ukraine.

For some nations, the path from non-coercive civil religion to coercive political religion was long. For the Germans, for instance, it took more than a century to make the journey "from Kant to Krupp."[43] For most Orthodox nations, however, this path was much shorter. Post-Soviet Russia walked it in under two years. Civil religions may not be as dangerous as political religions. Nevertheless, they are still risky as they can easily mutate to more violent forms.

---

42. Statement made by Tikhon Shevkunov on March 20, 2017: https://goo.gl/IhHPY3.
43. The title of the book by Léon Daudet, *Contre l'esprit allemand: de Kant à Krupp* [Against the German Spirit: From Kant to Krupp] (Paris: Bloud et Gay, 1915).

When a church embraces either civil or political religion, this is a political process. It inevitably alienates the church from its original mission and purpose and makes its Orthodoxy political and unorthodox. Churches agree to play a political role with the hope of enhancing their mission among the people. The result, however, in most cases is the opposite of what was expected: political Orthodoxy eventually undermines people's trust in the church. The governments that welcome the political engagement of the church also initially have high hopes. Usually they do so when they face crises of legitimacy. They expect that politicized religion can help improve their popularity among the people. However, this often ends up as dictatorship and eventually in a change of regime. Political Orthodoxy can be beneficial for both the church and state in the short run, but it always frustrates them in the long run.

3

——

Orthodox Ideologies: Antimodernism, Monarchism, and Conservatism

All Orthodox civil and political religions have an ideological, secular basis. These religions are byproducts of the era of secularization. Secularization both benefited and damaged the church. Among its benefits were separation from the state and the reemergence of a distinct ecclesial "self."[1] Ideologization of the church, however, is a damaging side effect of secularization. It diverts the church from leading people toward God to leading them toward a political goal. In other words, ideology turns the church from the instrument of salvation to a political instrument. An ideologized church thus goes against its own nature and purpose. In such churches, ideologemes, or particular ideological beliefs, become more prevalent and influential than doctrinal Christian beliefs. Ideologemes reflecting the liberal agenda of modern Western societies are more frequent in the churches of Reformation and less popular in the Orthodox churches, which prefer conservative ideologemes. Antimodernism, monarchism, and conservatism are three significant ideologies whose roles in the Orthodox church exemplify the negative effects of secularization. In what follows, we study them in the cases of Greece, Romania, and Russia.

Antimodernism

Orthodox opposition to the modernization of society is not unique—it coheres with similar resistance in other confessions. The Catholic Church had its own war on what it used to call the "heresy of modernism." This war was particularly intense under Pius IX (1792–1878) and Pius X (1835–1914). The former included forms of modernism in the *Syllabus errorum* (1864), and the

1. See Cyril Hovorun, *Meta-Ecclesiology: Chronicles on Church Awareness* (New York: Palgrave Macmillan, 2015), 79–94.

latter condemned modernism as heresy in *Lamentabili sane exitu* and *Pascendi Dominici gregis* (1907). In 1910, Pius X introduced an antimodernist oath for all bishops, priests, and academics.

In the Protestant milieu, the fight against modernism took the form of fundamentalism. The American Baptist pastor Curtis Lee Laws (1868–1946), who coined the term *fundamentalist* in 1920, defined antimodernism as

> a protest against that rationalistic interpretation of Christianity which seeks to discredit supernaturalism. This rationalism, when full grown, scorns the miracles of the Old Testament, sets aside the virgin birth of our Lord as a thing unbelievable, laughs at the credulity of those who accept many of the New Testament miracles, reduces the resurrection of our Lord to the fact that death did not end his existence, and sweeps away the promises of his second coming as an idle dream. It matters not by what name these modernists are known. The simple fact is that, in robbing Christianity of its supernatural content, they are undermining the very foundations of our holy religion. They boast that they are strengthening the foundations and making Christianity more rational and more acceptable to thoughtful people. Christianity is rooted and grounded in supernaturalism, and when robbed of supernaturalism it ceases to be a religion and becomes an exalted system of ethics.[2]

2. Curtis Lee Laws, "Herald and Presbyter," *The Watchman Examiner*, July 19, 1922.

The antimodernist sentiment of Piuses's Catholicism and Laws's fundamentalism echo in their contemporary Orthodox theologians, such as the Archbishop of Poltava Feofan Bystrov (1872–1940), who also opposed "modernism."[3] Feofan was one of the founding fathers of the Russian Orthodox Church Outside Russia (ROCOR), which made an antimodernist agenda a part of its creed.

In the Balkans, the global antimodernist movement in the beginning of the twentieth century was embodied in the group of schismatic churches known as "Old-calendarists."[4] These churches refused to accept the Gregorian ("new") calendar, to which most local Orthodox churches had switched in the 1920s. Besides the issue of liturgical calendar, they also became connected through their shared antimodernism.

Orthodox ecclesiology, which measures the church in jurisdictions,[5] makes possible turning an ideological movement into an autonomous jurisdiction. The antimodernist "Old-calendarist" jurisdictions, which can be also identified as fundamentalist jurisdictions, are

3. See his letter 72 to the Archbishop Averkiy Taushev from December 6, 1930, in *Pis'ma Arkhiepiskopa Feofana Poltavskogo i Pereyaslavskogo* [Letters from Archbishop Feofan of Poltava and Pereyaslav] (Jordanville, NY: Holy Trinity Publications, 1976).

4. In Greece, they are known as Παλαιοημερολογίτες ("Old-calendarists"), in Romania as *Biserica Ortodoxă de Stil Vechi din România* ("Old Style Orthodox Church in Romania"), and in Bulgaria as *Българска Православна Старостилна Църква* ("Bulgarian Old Style Orthodox Church").

5. See Cyril Hovorun, *Scaffolds of the Church: Towards Poststructural Ecclesiology* (Eugene, OR: Cascade, 2017), 50–87.

known as "Genuine Orthodox Christians" (Γνήσιοι Ορθόδοξοι Χριστιανοί) or "True Orthodox Churches" (Истинные Православные Церкви). They claim that they are "genuine" and "true" because they do not accept ecumenism. They condemn other Orthodox churches that participate in the ecumenical movement.

Anti-ecumenism, which is held by the "genuine" jurisdictions and some groups in the canonical jurisdictions, constitutes part of the antimodernist sentiment. It is also a form of political conservatism articulated in theological language. For those groups, ecumenism stands for liberalism and globalization. They believe that ecumenism compromises the unworldly nature of the church. For this reason, the anti-ecumenical churches often label the canonical churches that participate in the ecumenical movement as "world Orthodoxy" (мировое православие).

Antimodernist currents also flow through mainstream Orthodox jurisdictions. In the Russian Orthodox Church, for instance, a group of antimodernists run a website called "Antimodernism" (Antimodern.ru). It has the format of Wikipedia and calls itself "Wiki-Antimodern." This website defines modernism as

a holistic world view, which tries to morally justify and intellectually substantiate the lack of faith in God, of the dogmatic faith in the Nicene Creed. . . . Historically, modernism emerged from three ideological directions:

1) adaptation of religious views to the modern way of thinking; 2) the doctrine that God is immanent to man and that the cultural progress of mankind is the Revelation of God; 3) the belief that civilization is progressing towards the Kingdom of God.[6]

The All-Greek Orthodox Union (Πανελλήνιος Ὀρθόδοξος Ἕνωσις), which represents the ultra-conservative wing of the mainstream Orthodox Greek jurisdiction, publishes an antimodernist newspaper, *The Orthodox Press* (Ὀρθόδοξος Τύπος). Major contemporary proponents of Greek antimodernism are the Metropolitan of Piraeus Serafim Mentzelopoulos and priest Theodoros Zisis.

A common feature of antimodernist/fundamentalist programs across varied Christian confessions is their use of political instruments to achieve their goals. Ian Lustick's definition of fundamentalism as "a style of political participation characterized by unusually close and direct links between one's fundamental beliefs and political behavior designed to effect radical change" aptly describes this commonality.[7] When antimodernists have an opportunity, they apply direct political action. This struggle can be violent, and antimodernists then may become terrorists.[8]

Russian aggression against Ukraine is an example of a transformation from antimodernism to terrorism.

6. Antimodernism, accessed April 23, 2018, https://tinyurl.com/y6u2tcmz.
7. Ian Lustick, *For the Land and the Lord: Jewish Fundamentalism in Israel* (New York: Council on Foreign Relations, 1988), 5.
8. See Lucy Sargisson, *Fool's Gold?* (New York: Palgrave Macmillan, 2012), 50.

Some key figures of the Russian military campaign in Ukraine fulfill the classical criteria of fundamentalism. One of them is Konstantin Malofeyev, a major figure in the annexation of Crimea and the invasion of Russian troops in the Donbas region. Malofeyev is an Orthodox fundamentalist and antimodernist. During the war in Ukraine, one of his employees, Igor Girkin, became a field commander whose troops captured the city of Sloviansk in the eastern Ukraine. Girkin's press secretary was Igor Druz', an Orthodox believer who expressed sympathy with the fundamentalist groups even in other confessions. For example, he endorsed the Lefebvrist movement in the Catholic Church.[9] The "Antimodernism" website published a significant number of materials praising the Russian war in Ukraine. It presents the war as pursuing the same goals that the Orthodox antimodernists stand for. The violent doctrine of the "Russian world," which is an ideological engine of the war in Ukraine, contains among other things an explicit antimodernist agenda. It advocates archaic sociopolitical forms and opposes the advance of the post-Soviet societies towards democracy.

The war that Russia launched against Ukraine in 2014 was triggered by the choice of the majority of

---

9. Игорь Друзь, "Ekumenicheskiye kontaksty RPTs—udar po natsional'noy bezopasnosti Rossii" [The Ecumenical Contacts of the Russian Orthodox Church Is a Threat for the National Security of Russia], February 11, 2016, https://tinyurl.com/y72ep4md.

the Ukrainian people to move toward integration with the West. From the perspective of the doctrine of the "Russian world," this was a betrayal of Russian civilization for the sake of the West. The Russian military campaign in Ukraine was led under anti-Western banners—for the "holy Rus'" and against the "godless West." By employing anti-Western rhetoric, the Russian propaganda hit the nerve of traditional Orthodox Occidentalism.

Since at least the Fourth Crusade and the capture of Constantinople by Western troops (1204), Orthodox churches have developed a complex system of prejudices against the West. During the centuries that followed, some of these prejudices contributed to the formation of the confessional identity of Orthodox. In this identity, theology and geography were conflated: Orthodox faith became interpreted in terms of Occidentalism—mistrust, even dehumanization, of the West.[10] As George Demacopoulos and Aristotle Papanikolaou have remarked, "The categories of East and West are . . . almost always projections of an imagined difference."[11] Occidentalism is a relatively recent development of the anti-Western resentment. Before the secular age of modernity, this resentment had a

---

10. See Couze Venn, *Occidentalism* (London: Sage, 2000); Avishai Margalit and Ian Buruma, *Occidentalism: The West in the Eyes of Its Enemies* (New York: Penguin, 2014).
11. George Demacopoulos and Aristotle Papanikolaou, eds., "Orthodox Naming of the Other: A Postcolonial Approach," in *Orthodox Constructions of the West* (New York: Fordham University Press, 2013), 2.

form of confessionalism. In the period of modernity, it turned to an ideology. The ideology of Occidentalism is often shared even by those people in the Orthodox countries who are not religious anymore. To them, it substituted for Orthodoxy. The word "Orthodoxy," nevertheless, is still often used for what in reality is secularized Occidentalism.

Russia plays a crucial role in sustaining modern global Occidentalism among the Orthodox. This seemingly Orthodox state is believed by many Orthodox Christians worldwide to be a necessary counterweight to the Western world. According to a Pew study, Armenia (83 percent) and Serbia (80 percent) are among the top countries that hold this idea. The Armenians still suffer from the trauma of genocide and believe that Russia can protect them. Serbians suffer from the phantom pains of losing their own neo-communist empire under Slobodan Milošević (1965–2006). In Ukraine only 22 percent of people believe in Orthodox Occidentalism, largely because the Russian "protectionism" against the West turned into annexation of Crimea and a war in the east of Ukraine.

Indeed, the war in Ukraine was instigated by anti-Western resentment amplified by Russian state propaganda. This propaganda urged many Orthodox Christians and anti-Westerners from many countries, including Western nations, to go to Donbas and fight at an imagined anti-Western front. In a video clip about the "Russian Orthodox Army" fighting in the Donbas,[12] members of this military group testify that they fight against the antichrist coming from the West. Occidentalism is also a reason many Orthodox Christians worldwide support the military actions of Russia in Ukraine. For them, this is a holy war of the East against the West. They do not acknowledge that most of those killed in this war on both sides are Orthodox Christians. Christian ethics and Orthodox solidarity appear to be overwhelmed by anti-Western sentiment. Figures from Pew research indicate how much stronger Occidentalism is than Orthodox solidarity and ethos, and over ten thousand human lives lost in the Russo-Ukrainian war demonstrate the danger of this sort of political Orthodoxy.

This is not the only paradox of Orthodox Occidentalism. It has paradoxically allied itself with Western antimodernists, including American neo-fundamentalist and alt-right groups. The latter are often motivated by Orientalism—another set of prejudices, this time against the East—both Middle and Far East. Thus two opposite doctrines, Occidentalism and Orientalism, form an awkward alliance that sows seeds of chaos and hatred between peoples who identify themselves with different sides of horizon. These two seemingly opposite groups come together in a common struggle against modernism, globalism, and democracy.

12. "Russkaya Pravoslavnaya Armiya, iyul' 2014 g." [Russian Orthodox Army, July 2014], YouTube video, 8:22, uploaded by Andrey Smirnov, July 23, 2014, https://tinyurl.com/yda4cs9b.

Antidemocratism is a key part of the larger anti-modernist agenda. Given that democracy comes from the West, it frequently converges with Occidentalism. Chronologically, the Orthodox antidemocratic movement coincided with the rise of the global antimodernism. In the era when most Catholic, Protestant, and Orthodox antimodernist movements emerged, the Russian Saint Ioann of Kronstadt (1829–1909) reportedly uttered a dictum that became a motto of Orthodox antidemocratism: "Democracy is in hell, in Heaven there is a kingdom." Much like the beginning of the twentieth century, at the beginning of the twenty-first century in Russia democracy was presented as a product of the secularization, liberalization, and Westernization of traditional society. It is perceived as a threat to Orthodoxy. Many Russian Orthodox invest their strength in resisting democracy. They are encouraged to do so by pragmatic political elites who perceive democracy as a threat to their kleptocratic hold on Russia with its human and natural resources. The political Orthodoxy of antidemocratism thus enhances the vicious circle of the Russian plutocracy, which steals from the Russian people while at the same time making the Russian people appreciate and even defend being robbed.

Monarchism

Russian bishop Serafim Sobolev (1881–1950) believed that democracy is a diabolical political system. He argued that "both the republican and constitutional forms of government do not only lack being established by God, but their very existence begins with rejection [of God]."[13] His book, *The Russian Ideology,* can be seen as a manifesto of Russian civil religion. In Serafim's interpretation, monarchy constitutes the core of this religion. He rendered monarchy, in metaphysical terms, as the only political system that reflects the divine order of being. A tsar, for Serafim, was "a head and a soul of the Russian people."[14] He represented God and was expected to be venerated by people in a God-like manner. The Russian people must "love the tsar, who is the Anointed One by God, sacrifice themselves, suffer and die for the tsar, and look at him as a reflection of the glory and grandeur of God."[15]

These views echo the credo of the Black Hundred movement as well as other monarchist groups that flourished in Russia in the beginning of the twentieth century. They were strict in protecting the absolute sovereignty of tsars and criticized any form of compromising this sovereignty. For instance, they regarded

13. Serafim Sobolev, *Russkaya Ideologiya* [The Russian Ideology] (Moscow: Sofia, 1939).
14. Sobolev, *Russkaya Ideologiya* [The Russian Ideology].
15. Sobolev, *Russkaya Ideologiya* [The Russian Ideology].

even conservatives who wanted to counterbalance monarchical power by a constitutional process as their enemies.[16]

For the Black Hundred and for many Russian Orthodox who were sympathetic toward this organization, democracy was a heresy. The only Orthodoxy they admitted was a monarchical system of governance. This sort of Orthodoxy reemerged after the collapse of the Soviet Union and became a creed for multiple monarchical organizations that mushroomed first spontaneously and later with the support from the church and the state. As early as 1989, a Slavic Council (Славянский Собор) was founded that unified different nationalist groups and claimed succession to the Black Hundred. Other post-Soviet monarchical groups followed soon, also claiming kinship with the pre-Bolshevik monarchical groups. Thus, the Union of the Russian People (Союз Русского народа) was reestablished in 2005. All these groups are curated by the Orthodox clergy, such as, for instance, monastic priests Nikon Belavenets and Kirill Sakharov.

Kirill Sakharov is the leader of a movement that promotes collective penance for the murder of the Tsar Nikolai II by the Bolsheviks in 1918. People who belong to this movement come together to worship with special petitions asking God to forgive them if it were them and not Bolsheviks who murdered the

16. See Y. I. Kiryanov, *Pravyye partii v Rossii, 1911-1917* [*The Right-Wing Parties in Russia, 1911-1917*] (Moscow: Russian Political Encyclopedia Press, 2001), 4.

Romanovs. Theoretical foundations of this rite were laid down by Serafim Sobolev, who wrote: "There is no need to prove how horrible it is to . . . overthrow the tsar by his subjects. In this, the violation of the divine commandment reaches its highest degree of crime, and entails the death of the State. This . . . has been done by the Russian people."[17]

On these theological premises, Serafim called upon the Russian people to repent "for their grave sin of rebellion against monarchy."[18] By its form, this resembles the biblical collective repentance for the "sins of the people." However, in modern political circumstances in Russia, it effectively contributes to the Russian authoritarianism. In this capacity, the "all-people's repentance" (всенародное покаяние) and the cult of Tsar Nikolai constitute an intrinsic part of post-Soviet civil/political religion.

As with other manifestations of this religion, this one eventually became more coercive. A significant number of those who participated in the "all-people's repentance" took weapons in their hands and went to fight to expand Putin's monarchy into Ukraine. For example, one of the protagonists of the annexation of Crimea, the former Prosecutor General of the Ukrainian Republic of Crimea, Natalia Poklonskaya, is a devoted follower of the "penance movement." According to testimony of Igor Druz', an Orthodox fundamen-

17. Sobolev, *Russkaya Ideologiya* [The Russian Ideology].
18. Sobolev, *Russkaya Ideologiya* [The Russian Ideology].

talist who turned to a pro-Russian terrorist in the east of Ukraine, "the core of rebellion in *Novorossiya* [the Russian propaganda uses this name for the occupied territories in the eastern Ukraine] consisted of the Orthodox monarchists."[19]

The belief of post-Soviet monarchists in monarchy is absolute. They treat it as if it was the kingdom of God. There is, however, a more pragmatic line of thought in Russian monarchism. It was articulated by Russian philosopher Ivan Ilyin. Ilyin believed that democracy is not suitable for all cultures. In his opinion, Russian culture is best served by monarchy.[20] Ilyin wrote in emigration during the harshest decades of the Soviet regime. Nevertheless, he was convinced that this regime would eventually fall. After its collapse, he envisaged a restoration not of democracy but of monarchy. Notably, he understood monarchy not necessarily as a hereditary succession of tsars but generally as a rule of one man. Perhaps for this reason Ilyin is one of Vladimir Putin's favorite philosophers.

In Romania, similar ideas were propagated by Nichifor Crainic (1889–1972), one of the ideologues of the "Iron Guard," who followed the line of Russian thought.[21] He argued that Romania is naturally

---

19. A podcast of the Service of Spiritual Security, April 11, 2018, http://youtu.be/-BV1oaiteWU.
20. See Ivan Ilyin, *O gryaduschey Rossii: izbrannyye statyi* [On the Coming Russia: Selected Articles] (Moscow: Voyenizdat, 1993), 28.
21. See Peter Sugar, ed., *Eastern European Nationalism in the Twentieth Century* (Lanham, MD: American University Press, 1995), 288.

monarchical and interpreted Romanian monarchism as "ethnocracy," which is the opposite of democracy:

> Our state is monarchical throughout its entire history. The monarchy is the principle of its continuity. The crown of the Romanian King symbolizes the glory of the people and the permanence of Romanian consciousness. The ethnocratic state differs profoundly from the democratic state. The democratic state is based on the number of population, without racial or religious distinction. The foundation of the ethnocratic state is the Romanian soil and people. The democratic state is more of a registration office. The ethnocratic state is the will for power and the increase of the Romanian people. Its principal factors are: soil, blood, soul, and faith.[22]

In Romania, there was also a more metaphysical interpretation of monarchy close to the one preached by Archbishop Serafim Sobolev. Metropolitan Andrei Şaguna, a key ideologue and himself a symbol of the Romanian civil religion, advocated monarchy for the sake of monarchy, even if it was not Orthodox, as in the case of the Habsburg Empire.[23]

These sympathies for monarchy have survived all the changes of the political regimes in Russia and some

---

22. Nichifor Crainic, "Programul statului etnocratic" [The Program of the Ethnocratic State], in *Ortodoxie şi etnocratie* [Orthodoxy and Ethnocracy] (Bucharest: Cugetarea, 1938), 283–84, 310–11. Translated by James P. Niessen in Sugar, *Eastern European Nationalism*, 275.

23. See Cristian Romocea, *Church and State: Religious Nationalism and State Identification in Post-Communist Romania* (London: Continuum, 2011), 117.

other Orthodox countries. This has been confirmed by Pew research. The Republic of Moldova, which is historically and culturally close to both Romania and Russia, has the largest number of those who prefer non-democratic (i.e., monarchical) forms of government: 44 percent. In Russia, the percentage is a bit lower: 41 percent. In Romania, however, there are more who support democracy (52 percent) than those who either support non-democratic governance (28 percent) or do not care (17 percent).[24]

In Greece, the period of transition from monarchy to democracy was marked by heated debates about whether monarchy was the only "Orthodox" form of political rule. The anathema against the prime minister of Greece, Eleftherios Venizelos (1864–1936), epitomized the conflict surrounding the two forms of government.[25] This anathema occurred in the context of the national divide, when part of the Greek establishment supported Venizelos, who resided in Thessaloniki with his government. The rest of the establishment, opposed to Venizelos, supported King Konstantinos (1868–1923), who resided in Athens. The synod of the autocephalous Greek church, with the Archbishop of Athens Theoklitos (1848–1931) as its president,

24. Pew Research Center, "Religious Belief and National Belonging in Central and Eastern Europe," Pew Research Center, May 10, 2017, 141, https://tinyurl.com/y9ejlfx9.

25. See Andreas Nanakis, "Venizelos and Church-State Relations," in *Eleftherios Venizelos: The Trials of Statesmanship* (Edinburgh: Edinburgh University Press, 2006), 358–61.

supported the king and officially anathematized the prime minister. This was effectively an act against the office, which stood for republicanism and undermined monarchy, and not so much an act against Venizelos personally. As a person and politician, he was not against the church. Moreover, he enjoyed wide support of a faction within the Greek hierarchy, which was in the orbit of the Patriarchate of Constantinople.

To enhance the anathema publicly, the synod of the independent Greek church organized a religious procession on December 12, 1916. Participants in this procession made symbolic gestures by throwing stones and repeating the anathema against Venizelos. The ritual was similar to the anathema proclaimed two centuries earlier against the Ukrainian het'man Ivan Mazepa. In both cases, anathema was a political act vested in ecclesial robes.

It would be an exaggeration to say that the Orthodox church always supports monarchy. Its current official leadership should be credited with a more balanced take on the issue. For instance, in 2000 the Russian Orthodox Church adopted *The Basis of the Social Concept*, which declared the neutrality of the church to any form of political rule, as an official document articulating the church's teaching on church-state relations.[26] This was a response from the official church to the monarchists that wanted the church to confirm a pref-

26. Russian Orthodox Church, *The Basis of the Social Concept* 3.7, https://tinyurl.com/y8bdzw4y.

erence for monarchy. In the same vein, the Romanian church supports republicanism in Romania, from which it gets many benefits. The Greek hierarchs are even less inclined to the restoration of monarchy. In contrast to other Orthodox countries, democracy is not something brought to Greece from abroad. Ancient Athenian democracy constitutes an important part of the modern Greek national narrative. As a result, Greek civil religion is neither anti-democratic nor monarchist. This can be seen from Pew research, where Greece has the highest support for democracy among Orthodox countries at 77 percent.[27]

Conservatism

While the church officially proclaims its neutrality with regards to the forms of governance, some church officials have proclaimed the ideology of conservatism as optimal for Orthodoxy. For instance, the Patriarch of Moscow Kirill, in his Christmas interview on the state TV channel "Russia-1" on January 7, 2014, stated that "conservatism is religious in its nature" while "liberalism is a freedom understood in the wrong way."[28] During his meeting with the students of the theological academy in Kyiv in July 2009, he presented liberalism as a device welcoming the antichrist.[29]

27. Pew Research Center, "Religious Belief and National Belonging," 141.
28. "Christmas Interview of His Holiness Patriarch Kirill," Russia-1, January 7, 2014, https://tinyurl.com/ycbnauv2.

Conservatism underpins the other ideologemes —antimodernism and monarchism—that we have considered so far. In a secular society, the ideology of conservatism wrestles open-handedly with its main antagonist—liberalism. In the church, the political ideology of conservatism dresses itself in the fancy costume of monarchism. Antimodernism and anti-ecumenism can also be regarded as projections of conservatism. Conservatism thus bridges all modern political Orthodoxies and could be seen as their main ideological platform.

Those who identify Orthodoxy with conservatism dramatically narrow Christianity. Such a reduction makes the church similar to a political party. Propagation of conservatism as a new Orthodoxy also reduces the wide array of ideological platforms to the binary of conservatism-liberalism. This binary developed primarily in the American political context and reflects the American-style system of two parties. Those who praise conservatism as Orthodoxy and condemn liberalism as heresy effectively think in terms of American political culture and lock their churches into its framework. They conscript the manpower of their churches for American culture wars. These wars have been fought between Democrats and Republicans at least from the era of Jefferson.[30] Orthodox churches have

---

29. "Speech of His Holiness Patriarch Kirill," Kyiv-Pechersk Lavra, July 29, 2009, https://tinyurl.com/y7bp93fh.
30. See Stephen R. Prothero, *Why Liberals Win the Culture Wars (Even When They*

also participated in such wars since the beginning of modernity.

The earliest Orthodox culture war was fought in Greece in the last years of the eighteenth through the first decades of the nineteenth century. It divided the church by the criteria of one's attitude toward the Enlightenment, the political independence of the Greek nation, and the autocephaly of the Greek church. Among the founding fathers of the Greek Enlightenment was the bishop of Kherson (in Ukraine) Eugenios Voulgaris (1716–1806). He translated Voltaire into Greek and directed a theological academy on the conservative Mount Athos (Ἀθωνιάδα Ἀκαδημία). A considerable number of lower clergy supported liberal ideas as well, including the Athonite priest-monk Veniamin from Lesbos (1759–1824); priest-monks Neophytos Doukas (1760–1845), Anthimos Gazis (1764–1828), Stefanos Dougas (d. 1830), Athanasios Psalidas (1767–1829), Konstantinos Koumas (1777–1836), Neophytos Vamvas (1770–1855), Theophilos Kaïris (1784–1853); and the highly influential archimandrite Theoklitos Pharmakidis (1784–1860). Pharmakidis shared the ideas of Enlightenment, supported Greek independence, and helped construct the autocephaly of the Greek church.

The key figure of the Greek Enlightenment, Adamantios Koraïs (1748–1833), also wanted the Greek

Lose Elections): The Battles That Define America from Jefferson's Heresies to Gay Marriage (New York: HarperOne, 2016).

nation and church to be independent. Koraïs studied theology in Smyrna and later went to Montpellier in France to study medicine, with financial support from the former bishop of Corinth Makarios Notaras (1731–1805). Makarios helped Koraïs print his translation of the *Catechism* of the Metropolitan Platon of Moscow (1782). Koraïs also published his own theological treatises: *The Synopsis of the Holy History and a Catechism* (Venice, 1783) and *The Little Catechism* (Venice, 1783). In the first years of the nineteenth century, Koraïs began composing political pamphlets in support of the Enlightenment. He particularly promoted the concept of *Metakinosis* (Μετακίνωσις), which he designed himself. According to this concept, ancient Greek culture influenced contemporary European civilization through the ideas of the Renaissance. Now this culture needs to be brought back to Greece in the form of the Enlightenment.

Conservative clergy opposed Koraïs's ideas, with the hieromonk Athanasios from the Aegean isle of Paros (1721/22–1813) leading the anti-Enlightenment "resistance." Athanasios was a prominent figure in the intellectual and spiritual life of Ottoman Greece and was declared a saint by the Ecumenical Patriarchate. He completely rebuked the Enlightenment in both French and Greek forms, which were for him tricks of the antichrist.[31] He declared liberal philosophy completely wrong, and called it φιλοζοφία—"love for darkness."[32]

While arguing against Western ideologies, Athanasios constructed his own ideology that reduced the Christian ethos to conservatism. Another feature of Athanasios's ideological schema is its opposition to the West. Athanasios's works constitute one of the earliest instances in the modern era of a political ideology disguised as an Orthodox doctrine. This ideology effectively substituted theology. It is remarkable, however, that his ideological concerns were not shared by all his fellow Kollyvades—the participants in the movement of spiritual and liturgical renaissance that lasted from the middle of eighteenth century to the 1820s.[33] Athanasios was a part of this movement. However, other leaders of the Kollyvadic movement, Makarios Notaras and Nikodimos the Hagiorite (1749–1809), did not seem to endorse the ideological reductions of Athanasios. On the contrary, Makarios supported Adamantios Koraïs in his studies in France, and Nikodimos actively borrowed from the books of Jesuit

31. See Athanasios Parios, *Peri tis alithus filosofias, i antifonisis pros ton paralogon zilon ton apo tis Evropis erkhomenon filosofon ke epi afilosofia to imeteron genos anoitos iktironton* [On the True Philosophy, or the Response to the Mad Zeal of the Philosophers Coming from Europe and On the Non-Philosophy, Which Is Unwisely Promoted to Our People] (Triest, 1802), 70.
32. Parios, *Peri tis alithus filosofias* [On the True Philosophy], 40.
33. See Serhiy (Cyril) Hovorun, "Dvizheniye kollivadov v Gretsii, yego svyaz' s isikhazmom i vliyaniye na sovremennuyu zhizn' Elladskoy Tserkvi" [The Movement of the Kollyvades in Greece, Its Relationship to the Hesychasm, and Its Influence on the Modern Life of the Greek Church] (Thesis, Kyiv Theological Academy, 1998).

theology and spirituality for his own writings.[34] Although his treatises were anti-Latin, there are no indications that they were anti-Western—something that can be regarded as a hallmark distinguishing theology from ideology.

An even more heated culture war was waged among the factions of the Russian church after the Bolshevik revolution in October 1917. The one Orthodox church of the Romanovs' empire was torn to several pieces. These pieces became reshuffled around ideologies and thus formed ideological jurisdictions: the Moscow Patriarchate, the Russian Exarchate in Western Europe under the Ecumenical Patriarchate, and the Russian Orthodox Church Outside Russia.

The political landscape of the Russian empire during the twenty years before its collapse could be divided in three areas: (1) a conservative one with various monarchist movements and organizations such as the Black Hundred; (2) a liberal one with the Party of Constitutional Democrats in its center; and (3) the socialists, who upheld a radical leftist agenda and applied revolutionary methods of class struggle. In October 1917, the third group seized political power, and its most radical wing, the Bolsheviks, established the dictatorship of the proletarians. The other two groups either emi-

34. See Cyril Hovorun, "St. Nikodemos the Hagiorite (1749–1809)," in *The Encyclopedia of Eastern Orthodox Christianity*, ed. John A. McGuckin, vol. 2 (Malden, MA: Blackwell, 2011).

grated or were gradually exterminated by the Bolsheviks.

After emigrating, the conservative and liberal groups remained separate from each other. They even chose different countries as their new homes. The liberals anchored in Czechoslovakia, France, and the United States, while the conservatives preferred Yugoslavia, China, and Argentina. In their new countries, both groups established their own political and civil organizations, presses, publishing houses, universities, and churches.

Dozens of bishops and priests left Russia following their fleeing flock. Once they moved, they faced a need to establish new ecclesial structures as they could not maintain unity with their center in Moscow. However, they failed to set up a single structure with one ecclesial center. Instead, they established two ecclesial structures, which reflected the two major ideological platforms of the Russian emigration. The conservative group established its synod in Serbia and elected as its primate Metropolitan Antoniy Khrapovitskiy (1863–1936). The liberal group, under the leadership of Metropolitan Yevlogiy Georgievskiy (1868–1946), joined the Ecumenical Patriarchate in 1931, in the capacity of a self-ruling exarchate—several parishes managed by the representative of the patriarch. Thus the three major parts of the Russian Orthodox Church associated themselves with three major ideological platforms that had emerged in the last years of the

Russian empire. The Moscow Patriarchate aligned with the socialist regime in the Soviet Union, especially after Metropolitan Sergiy issued his infamous declaration of loyalty in 1927. What became the Russian Orthodox Church Outside Russia (ROCOR) merged with the monarchist and conservative movements. And what became the Russian exarchate in Western Europe in unity with the Ecumenical Patriarchate largely preserved the liberal political preferences of the majority of its flock.

The ideological divisions between these three churches were deep. In 1930, Metropolitan Yevlogiy (the Russian exarchate in Paris) was deposed by Metropolitan Sergiy (Moscow) because he participated in the prayer for the church suffering in the Soviet Union. This prayer was held in London on the initiative of the Archbishop of Canterbury. In Moscow, it was interpreted as an anti-Soviet action, which the Russian liberals directed against Soviet Communists. The conservative ROCOR did not recognize the other two parts of the Russian church until its reunion with the Moscow Patriarchate in 2007. Before that, the ROCOR considered the Moscow Patriarchate a heretical organization and did not even accept its baptisms. At the same time, it did not hesitate to collaborate with the regimes that were against the Soviet Union, including the Nazis. Thus different parts of the Russian church opposed each other while simultaneously aligning themselves with non-Orthodox and even anti-Christian political regimes.

Liberal and conservative ideologies alike function as political Orthodoxies when a church identifies itself with a political agenda. The easiest way for the church to accommodate itself to a secular society is by embracing its dominant ideology: liberal in Western societies or conservative in Eastern ones. The positive effects of this, however, do not last long. The church usually fails to gain sustainable ideological support in its society and loses support from its traditional constituencies. Most important, the church loses itself because it reduces itself to something that is much narrower than Christianity—ideology.

4

Case Study: Anti-Semitism

Anti-Semitism is one of the oldest unorthodox Orthodoxies in Christianity. Before the Holocaust, the majority of Orthodox churches at least tolerated, if not openly promoted, various forms of anti-Semitism. Some churches, because anti-Semitism had become a tradition within the church, continued to tolerate anti-Semitism even after the Holocaust. In the modern era, however, anti-Semitism became more secular and thus somehow different from its premodern forms. During Christian antiquity and the Middle Ages, Christians rejected Jews because their *religion* was different from

117

Christianity. With the advance of modernity, Jews became rejected because they were a different *nation*. This shift marked the advance of secular thinking, which also affected the churches. Secularized anti-Semitism culminated in the Third Reich, where it turned into the most important political framework of the Nazi regime. Orthodox peoples contributed to this framework and adopted it for themselves. The Russian Orthodox royalists who escaped the Soviet regime brought with them to Germany some early ideas of political anti-Semitism. Other Orthodox nations, primarily the Romanian one, framed their own political regimes on the basis of Nazi-style anti-Semitism. Anti-Semitism in these cases became an intrinsic part of Orthodox civil/political religions.

The most common driving force behind anti-Semitism in late antiquity and the Middle Ages was the idea that Jews crucified Jesus. They thus betrayed God, who for centuries cared about the Jewish people and led them to accept the Messiah. This idea was articulated as early as the second century in patristic works such as the *Epistle to Barnabas* and the hymn on Pascha by Melito of Sardis. In the view of many Christians, the Jewish perception of God was deficient because they had not received the revelation of the Trinity. Christians also accused Jews of ritualism—paying attention to details of rituals instead of caring of God's commandments. They came to consider the entire Jewish spirituality as misleading. However, when Jews converted to Christianity, they were regarded as equals to other Christians in most cases. Jews who did not convert were exposed to violence and defamation.

Secularization brought some significant changes in the attitude of European states and public to Jews. On the one hand, Jews received more rights and became better integrated into European societies. They were treated as *individual* citizens with the same or almost the same rights as the rest of citizens. On the other hand, prejudices against Jews as a social group survived secularization. Now Jews were treated not so much as a religious but as an ethnic group. In the wake of the birth of the modern idea of nations, Judaism as a religious identity became more of an ethnic identity. As much as many Christians disliked Judaism as a religion in the period of late antiquity and the Middle Ages, they came to dislike Jews as a nation in the modern era. Now even Jewish conversion to Christianity did not save them from prejudices and suspicions, because in the era of nations, they remained *ethnic* Jews. Illustrative in this regard is the Romanian case. In medieval and early modern Romania, when Jews converted to Christianity, they became equal members of the local Christian communities. A convert could even become an Orthodox priest. The situation changed in the interwar period, when Romanian state laws prohibited the baptism of Jews. The legislators believed that Jews in this way tried avoiding deportations. The Romanian church endorsed these laws and in many cases did not respond to the requests of Jews for bap-tism.[1]

In the modern era, when the public space became more secular, anti-Semitism occupied a significant part of this space as a secular ideology. From theolog-ical, anti-Semitism turned more to political. It became one of many ideologies that grew with the process of secularization during the eighteenth and nineteenth centuries. As a secular ideology, it was reintroduced to many Christian churches, including the Orthodox ones. Similarly to other -isms of that epoch, it received its ideological name, "anti-Semitism." The German journalist Wilhelm Marr (1819–1904) coined this term in 1879.[2]

As mentioned earlier, the basic belief of premodern Christian anti-Semitism was that Jews crucified Jesus, developed a wrong idea about God, and had a wrong sort of spirituality. Both secular and religious anti-Semitisms in the modern era agreed on the opposite: Jews are not spiritual at all. Many religious and secular thinkers, especially those who were under the influ-ence of the German idealistic philosophy, accused the Jews of materialism. They believed that Jews under-mined the spiritual values of the European nations, and through economic instruments, they wanted to rule

1. See Ion Popa, *The Romanian Orthodox Church and the Holocaust* (Bloomington: Indiana University Press, 2017), 48–55.
2. See Anson Rabinbach and Sandeer L. Gilman, *The Third Reich Sourcebook* (Berkeley: University of California Press, 2013), 185.

the world. The idea about assumed Jewish materialism became one of the driving forces of modern anti-
Semitism, which made it different from its premodern
forms. Even theologians and church hierarchs adopted
the assumptions about Jewish materialism and
embraced conspiracy theories that Jews plot to ruin
any form of non-materialist spirituality. These
assumptions and theories also became a part of political Orthodoxies, even though they originated from secular sources.

Anti-Semitism penetrated many layers of secularized European society in the nineteenth century. It was
expressed in the philosophical language, music, art,
and literature of the time and was studied as a "science." Positivism invented a scientific anti-Semitism
and placed it to the center of racial science.[3] This "science" was a byproduct of contemporary groundbreak-
ing discoveries in biology. Although Charles Darwin
(1809–1882) was not anti-Semitic and his classic work
Origin of Species (1859) was not racial, the book nevertheless inspired several racial "scientists." For example, Francis Galton (1822–1911), a cousin of Charles
Darwin, founded eugenics in his study *Hereditary Genius*
(1869). On the basis of his studies in this field, Galton,
in an address to the International Congress of Demog-
raphy, suggested constraining the immigration of Jews

---

3. See Avner Falq, *Anti-Semitism: A History and Psychoanalysis of Contemporary Hatred* (Westport, CT: Praeger, 2008), 21–22.

and Chinese to the West to protect the purity of European races.[4]

Nineteenth-century Romanticism produced some artistic masterpieces with implicit anti-Semitic agendas. One of them was the opera *Parsifal* by Richard Wagner (1813–1883).[5] Wagner was a notorious anti-Semite. His basic idea was that German idealistic spirit is radically different from Jewish materialistic interests.[6] This idea stemmed from a more general framework of German idealist philosophy, which elevated *Geist* (spirit as opposed to matter) above utilitarianism. According to the ideologue of Nazism Alfred Rosenberg, German idealist philosophy, with its emphasis on spirit, was a rebellion against Jewish influence on Christianity. Indeed, several German idealist philosophers in the nineteenth century corroborated this thesis. Arthur Schopenhauer, for instance, asserted: "The true Jewish religion . . . is the crudest of all religions, since it is the only one that has absolutely no doctrine of immortality, nor even any trace of it . . . Judaism . . . is a religion without any metaphysical tendency."[7]

4. See William Brustein, *Roots of Hate: Anti-Semitism in Europe Before the Holocaust* (Cambridge: Cambridge University Press, 2010), 96–98.
5. See Joachim Köhler, *Wagner's Hitler: The Prophet and His Disciple*, trans. Ronald Taylor (Cambridge: Polity, 2000).
6. See his essay "Jewry in Music" (1850), in Paul Mendes-Flohr and Jehuda Reinharz, eds., *The Jew in the Modern World: A Documentary History* (New York: Oxford University Press, 2011), 303.
7. In Michael Kellogg, *The Russian Roots of Nazism: White Émigrés and the Making of National Socialism, 1917–1945* (Cambridge: Cambridge University Press, 2008), 21.

Some other German idealist philosophers presented Jews as a "nation," marking the transformation of religious anti-Semitism into its more secular version. Johann Gottlieb Fichte (1762–1814) stated characteristically: "A powerful, hostilely disposed nation is infiltrating almost every country in Europe. This nation is in a state of perpetual war with all these countries, severely afflicting their citizenry. I am referring to the Jewish nation . . . It is founded on the hatred of mankind."[8]

European anti-Semitic ideas, many of them developed in the secular framework, were appropriated by some Orthodox thinkers. They produced a political Orthodoxy that combined the contemporary secular animosity to Jews as a nation with the traditional Christian rejection of the Jewish religion. One such thinkers was Fyodor Dostoyevsky. He regarded Jews as an ethnic group that tends to isolate itself from other peoples. In contrast to them, the Russians, according to Dostoyevsky, have a universal mission that stems from their Orthodox religion. Dostoyevsky called the Jewish community "status in statu"—a state within the state.[9] He borrowed this phrase from Fichte, who had defined European Jewry as *Staat im Staate* ("a state within a state") in his 1793 essay.[10] At the same time,

---

8. "A State within a State," in Mendes-Flohr and Reinharz, *Jew in the Modern World*, 283.
9. "Status in statu," in letter 673 to A. Kovner, February 14, 1877, in Fyodor Dostoevsky, *Polnoye sobraniye sochineniy v tridtsati tomakh* [Complete Collection of Works in Thirty Volumes] (Leningrad: Nauka, 1986), 29:140.

Dostoyevsky stood for equal civil rights for Jews in Russia.[11] In this regard, his standpoint was not much different from that of Fichte or Wagner, who also supported equal civil rights for Jews in Germany. It seems that all these authors respected Jews as human beings but despised them as a nation. This sort of anti-Semitism became a part of civil religion in imperial Russia. In this form, anti-Semitism was a subject of everyday conversations and debates in literature salons but not a part of violent state policies.

In the last decades of the nineteenth century, Russian anti-Semitism became more violent, and the state stepped in to support it. Instrumental in this regard was Konstantin Pobedonostsev (1827–1907), who was a tutor of the tsars-to-be Alexander III (reigned 1881–94) and his son Nikolai II (reigned 1894–1917). From 1880 to 1905 he was the Ober-prokuror of the Holy Synod of the Russian church—the state-appointed chief executive officer in the church. He was also a key political figure in the government of Alexander III. Pobedonostsev thus defined the cultural and ecclesial policies of the Russian empire for several decades. In these policies, he often implemented his anti-Semitic views, which he also discussed in correspondence with Dostoyevsky.[12] Pobedonostsev pushed Alexander III and

10. Johann Gottlieb Fichte, *Beitrag zur Berichtigung der Urteile des Publikums über die französische Revolution (1793): Beigefügt ist die Rezension von Friedrich von Gentz (1794)* (Hamburg: Meiner, 1973), 113–16.

11. Dostoyevsky, *Polnoye sobraniye sochineniy* [Complete Collection of Works], 25:86.

later Nikolai II toward more restrictive measures against Jews. These measures included the Pale of Settlement: Jews were allowed to settle at a certain distance from big cities within a specially defined pale. Additionally, Jews were not allowed to hold certain official positions, and their business activities were under restrictive supervision by the authorities.

In the beginning of the twentieth century, state policies regarding Jews became even more restrictive. Newly established right-wing political parties officially included anti-Semitism in their political programs. Thus, in 1900, a Russian council was founded in St. Petersburg as a monarchical, conservative, Orthodox, and anti-Semitic party. Its purpose was to withstand "dark forces," in the words of its cofounder Vasiliy Velichko (1860–1904), by which he primarily meant Jews.

The Russian council was an elitist movement. A more popular monarchist party was established in 1905. It was called The Union of the Russian People. Tsar Nikolai II extended his personal patronage to the Union, which also received state funds and enjoyed police protection. It needed such protection because as an organizer of direct action, it was often involved in violence, including beating and killing activists disloyal to the monarchy. One year after its founding, the

12. Letter 808 to the Ober-prokuror of the Synod Konstantin Pobedonostsev, August 9, 1879, in Dostoyevsky, *Polnoye sobraniye sochineniy* [Complete Collection of Works], 30:104.

Union became the largest monarchical organization in the Russian empire. In the Russian Parliament, State Duma, it gained fifty-one places. The Russian Orthodox Church enthusiastically participated in the activities of the Union. Among its founders was an Orthodox priest-monk, Arseniy Alekseyev. In 1907, a widely respected priest, Ioann of Kronstadt, became an honorary member.

Some other right-wing political organizations grew in concert with the Union of the Russian People, such as the Union of the Archangel Michael, the Russian Monarchical Party, the Union of Struggle with Dissent, and the Council of United Nobility, among others—more than twenty of them.[13] Some of them comprised a movement, which was called Black Hundred. This name goes back to the Russian liberation movement in the beginning of the seventeenth century.

The Black Hundred targeted primarily leftist groups. Among its victims were students, educators, and intelligentsia. Jews also became a target—as an ethnic group, though, and not a social class. Even Jews who had converted to Christianity were not allowed to join the Black Hundred. This is an indication that its anti-Semitism was secular, even though it was rendered in religious terms.

The Black Hundred terrorized leftist groups with

---

13. See Y. I. Kiryanov, *Pravyye partii v Rossii, 1911–1917 gg.* [The Right-Wing Parties in Russia, 1911–1917] (Moscow: Russian Political Encyclopaedia Press, 2001), 5.

beatings and killings. It also instigated pogroms against Jews. The etymology of pogroms comes from the Russian *gromit'*—to smash out. Pogroms began with destroying Jewish shops and often ended with murders. For instance, in October 1905, the Black Hundred reportedly killed 1,622 people, of whom 711 were Jews.[14]

The Black Hundred, however, did not invent pogroms. An earlier documented instance of a pogrom happened, for example, in 1821 in Odessa and was committed by local Greeks. Its pretext was the murder of the Patriarch of Constantinople Grigorios V by Ottomans in Constantinople. When the body of the patriarch was brought to Odessa for a solemn funeral, the Greeks of the city decided that local Jews did not show sufficient respect and killed seventeen of them. The Greeks were helped by locals.[15] It seems, however, that the burial of the patriarch was not the reason but rather an excuse for the pogrom, which was most probably caused by competition between Greeks and Jews in trade.[16]

A new wave of pogroms was launched after the Tsar Alexander II was assassinated by Russian leftist Nikolai Rysakov in March 1881. The son of the murdered tsar, Alexander III, came to believe that Jews were to blame

14. Kellogg, *Russian Roots of Nazism*, 36.
15. See John Klier and Shlomo Lambroza, eds., *Pogroms: Anti-Jewish Violence in Modern Russian History* (Cambridge: Cambridge University Press, 2007), 17.
16. See Steven J. Zipperstein, *The Jews of Odessa: A Cultural History, 1794–1881* (Stanford: Stanford University Press, 2001), 119.

for social unrest and for the spread of radical socialist ideas, which eventually led to the assassination. Konstantin Pobedonostsev, who was a tutor and then an influential politician under Alexander III, instigated such conspiracy theories. The faithful subjects of the tsar sensed the grieving mood that engulfed the palace and began acting accordingly. A series of pogroms erupted throughout the southern regions of the empire in 1881–1884. The pogroms were widely supported, even by the public with university education. Only a few intellectuals openly condemned the pogroms, including the writer Mikhail Saltykov-Schedrin (1826–1889).

The next wave of pogroms was caused by Russian defeat in the war with Japan and the social turmoil that followed during the years 1903–1906. The pogroms in this period were triggered by rumors about the murder of Christian children by Jews—the so-called blood libel. Such was the case of the Chisinau pogrom in 1903, when Jews were accused of killing a Christian girl, who in reality had committed suicide. Another infamous cause, which became known internationally, was Menachem Beilis', who was accused of murdering a twelve-year-old boy Andrey Yuschinskiy in Kyiv.[17] Beilis was also not proved guilty, but his innocence did not prevent pogroms and did not stop the spread of conspiracy theories.

17. See Robert Weinberg, *Blood Libel in Late Imperial Russia: The Ritual Murder Trial of Mendel Beilis* (Bloomington: Indiana University Press, 2014).

The most infamous instance of anti-Semitic conspiracy theories was the forgery known as the *Protocols of the Elders of Zion*. The *Protocols* were fabricated, and their authenticity was never proven, but they became part of the propaganda believed by masses, and eventually drove them to political action and violence. The *Protocols of the Elders of Zion* look like actual protocols of sessions in which Jewish elders discussed how to establish Jewish rule over the world. The instruments of Jewish dominion would be, for example, the destruction of traditional Christian states, the support of free press, democracy, and human rights. In other words, the entire program of the modernization of society in the beginning of the twentieth century was presented as a Jewish conspiracy.

The origins of the *Protocols* are still unclear. Norman Cohn argued that they were fabricated by the Russian secret service (*Okhranka*). According to Cohn, they were first composed in French and then translated into Russian. Cohn argues that the person behind the forgery was Pyotr Rachkovskiy, who at the time of their appearance managed the network of Russian spies in Paris. Cohn based his version on the testimony of Russian historian Boris Nikolayevskiy (1887–1966).[18] However, as Nikolayevskiy wrote in a private letter to Vera Cohn, the Russian wife of Norman Cohn, this was false information.[19] Modern historians tend to

18. Norman Cohn, *Warrant for Genocide: The Myth of the Jewish World Conspiracy and the Protocols of the Elders of Zion* (London: Serif, 2006), 83–87.

conclude that the *Protocols* were forged not by Russian spies in Paris but in the Russian empire between April 1902 and August 1903, and were originally written in Russian before being translated into French.[20]

What is certain about the origins of the *Protocols* is that Sergei Nilus (1862–1929), a Russian spiritual writer and member of the Black Hundred, published them in the second edition of his book *The Great in the Small* (Великое в малом) in 1905.[21] This edition reached the royal palace. According to the information from the chief of the secret service in St. Petersburg Konstantin Globachev,[22] Tsar Nikolai II read the *Protocols* with great interest and a pen in hand. According to the same source, his prime minister Pyotr Stolypin (1862–1911) ordered an investigation on the origins of this document. Two experienced investigators from the secret

19. Kellogg, *Russian Roots of Nazism*, 58.

20. See Michael Hagemeister, "Der Mythos der 'Protokolle der Weisen von Zion'" [The Myth of the "Protocols of the Elders of Zion"], in *Verschworungstheorien: Anthropologische Konstanten—historische Varianten* [Contextual Theories: Anthropological Constants—Historical Variants], ed. Ute Caumanns and Matthias Niendorf (Osnabrück: Fibre, 2001), 96, 99.

21. Sergey Nilus, *Velikoye v malom i antikhrist kak blizkaya politicheskaya vozmozhnost'. Zapiski pravoslavnogo* [The Great in the Small and the Antichrist as a Close Political Possibility: Notes by an Orthodox] (Tsarskoye Selo: Red Cross Press, 1905). There are testimonies that the *Protocols* began circulating before 1905, in the winter of 1901–1902. See Yuriy Begunov, *Taynyye sily v istorii Rossii* [Secret Powers in the History of Russia] (Moscow: Institute of the Russian Civilization Press, 2016), 110–11.

22. See Rafaïl Ganelin, "Ot chernosotenstva k fashizmu" [From the Black Hundred Movement to Fascism], in *Ad Hominem: Pamyati Nikolaya Girenko* [Ad Hominem: In Memoriam of Nikolay Girenko] (St. Petersburg: МАЭ РАН, 2005), 253.

police proved that the *Protocols* were a forgery. This discovery disappointed Nikolai, but not his wife. Tsarina Alexandra (1872–1918) continued to believe in their authenticity and kept them even in the Ypatiev house near Yekaterinburg, where the royal family was executed by the Bolsheviks.[23]

The *Protocols* were transmitted to the West by Pyotr Shabelsky-Bork (1893–1952), a member of the Black Hundred. He was a devoted royalist and tried to rescue the Romanov family from their captivity in Yekaterinburg. He also participated in the anti-Bolshevik military campaign, which failed, and was rescued by Germans in the winter of 1918–1919.[24] With him, the *Protocols* were brought to Berlin. There, Shabelsky-Bork approached a publicist, who was also a German nationalist, Ludwig Müller von Hausen (1851–1926), with the text. Von Hausen arranged for the translation of the *Protocols* into German and their subsequent publication. Excerpts appeared first in 1920 in the *Völkischer Beobachter* ("People's Observer")—the official newspaper of the Nazi Party. The full document was published soon thereafter and became a bestseller. This publication of the *Protocols* resonated with antidemocratic and anti-Jewish sentiment in Germany and became a handbook for Nazis. Hitler himself read and referred to them in *Mein Kampf*.[25]

---

23. See Kellogg, *Russian Roots of Nazism*, 60.
24. Michael Kellogg found this information in a *Gestapo* report from April 1935. See Kellog, *Russian Roots of Nazism*, 63.

Russian and German anti-Semitisms share several commonalities. Both were based on the *völkische* ideology. At its core was the idea of a people. A people embodies the universal and obliging truth, which is more important than the interests and truths of an individual. This ideology appealed to the people's *Geist* (spirit), which transcends materialistic interests and helps a people survive various historical challenges, such as wars, foreign rule, and economic decline. Judaism, from the point of view of this ideology, is one such challenge. The Russian *völkische* ideology was embedded in the formula of the Russian statehood: "Orthodoxy, monarchy, *peopleness*" (православие, самодержавие, *народность*), which was proclaimed in the early nineteenth century. It was repeated in the middle of the same century by many intellectuals, including the Slavophiles and Dostoyevsky, who characteristically stated, "Russia is *völkische*" (Россия народна).[26] In the beginning of the twentieth century, this slogan was weaponized by the Black Hundred and used in pogroms.[27]

25. See Rabinbach and Gilman, *Third Reich Sourcebook*, 190. Heinrich Himmler exaggerated that "the *Führer* learned [the *Protocols*] by heart." In Hannah Arendt, *The Origins of Totalitarianism* (New York: Harcourt Brace Jovanovich, 1979), 360.

26. Dostoyevsky, *Polnoye sobraniye sochineniy* [Complete Collection of Works], 30:70.

27. In the beginning of the twenty-first century, *völkische* underpinned Russian aggression against Ukraine. For example, Alexandr Dugin, a proponent of the aggression, regards the *völkische* ideology a perennial pillar of the "Russian world." See "Aleksandr Dugin: Vizantiya—nashe vechnoye nachalo"

The *völkische* ideology featured a direct link to race theories. Although in Russia such theories were not developed to the same extent as in Western Europe, Russian anti-Semites upheld a form of proto-racism. Dostoyevsky, for instance, spoke of "breeds of people" (породы людей). Jews became such a breed that "mutated into something separate from the humankind as whole, and even something hostile to the humankind as whole."[28]

As mentioned earlier, both German and Russian anti-Semites associated Judaism with materialism and constructed their anti-Jewish attitude on the assumption that spirit is superior to matter. This attitude sprang from German idealistic philosophy and later became incorporated in the creed of Nazi political religion. Nazis juxtaposed presumably "materialistic" Jews with "spiritual" Germans, who, in the words of Houston Stewart Chamberlain (1855–1927), were so spiritual that "a race so profoundly and inwardly religious is unknown to history."[29] Russian anti-Semites employed the same contrast of the Russian people, the "bearer of God" (народ-богоносец), to the "godless" Jews. Dostoyevsky's hero Shatov in the novel *The Devils* stated in this regard that the Russian people are "the only

[Alexander Dugin: Byzantium—our Eternal Principle], YouTube video, 18:19, uploaded by Tsar'grad TV, November 26, 2015, https://tinyurl.com/y99nzt8n.

28. Letter 878 to Y. Abaza, June 15, 1880, in Dostoyevsky, *Polnoye sobraniye sochineniy* [Complete Collection of Works], 30:191.

29. See Kellogg, *Russian Roots of Nazism*, 24.

'god-bearing' people on earth."[30] In his political essays, Dostoyevsky repeated the idea that the Russians "bear God," and succeeded the Jews in this mission after the Jews rejected Jesus Christ.[31]

Similar line of thought can be observed in Romanian anti-Semitism, which became a part of both civil and political religions in Romania. A French ambassador to this country reported in 1900 that Romanian "anti-Semitism is more than just an idea, it is a passion common to politicians of all parties, the Orthodox church, and one could also add, to all the peasants, both Wallachian and Moldavian."[32] This is probably an exaggerated statement, which nevertheless reflects the depth and width of anti-Semitism in Romanian society and church. Student of Romanian anti-Semitism Ion Popa believes that it can be compared with only German anti-Semitism.[33]

As in Germany, many Romanian intellectuals supported and developed anti-Semitic ideas. Nicolae Iorga, for example, libeled Jews and justified pogroms in Bukovina and Bessarabia. In 1895, Iorga cofounded the International Anti-Semitic Alliance with his colleague Alexandru Constantin Cuza (1857–1947), a professor at

---

30. Fyodor Dostoyevsky, *The Devils*, trans. David Magarshack (London: Penguin, 1971), 253.
31. Dostoyevsky, *Polnoye sobraniye sochineniy* [Complete Collection of Works], 25:84–85.
32. In Peter Sugar, ed., *Eastern European Nationalism in the Twentieth Century* (Lanham, MD: American University Press, 1995), 281.
33. Popa, *Romanian Orthodox Church and the Holocaust*, 28.

the University of Iași. A. C. Cuza was one of the most notorious Romanian anti-Semites among the intellectuals. In 1910, he published a monograph, *The Reduction of the Christian Population and the Increase in the Number of Kikes*, where he promoted anti-Semitism as a "science." His "scientific" solution to the "Jewish question" meant a complete elimination of Jews from Romanian society.[34]

In his monograph, Cuza draws on the works of Chamberlain. His own writings became a basis for the Romanian movements of direct political action similar to the Black Hundred in Russia, such as the Iron Guard. Nichifor Crainic articulated the xenophobic and anti-Semitic principles of this organization:

> The soil of the Romanian people has today inhabitants of other races and faiths, as well. They came here through invasion (like the Hungarians), colonization (like the Germans), through crafty infiltration (like the Jews). Every one of them, fonder of its own people than ours, presents no guarantees of security for the official organism of the state. The Jews are a permanent danger for every national state.[35]

Another activist of the Iron Guard, Mihail Polohroniade (1906–1939), advocated for anti-Semitism to be

34. See Brustein, *Roots of Hate*, 155–56.
35. Nichifor Crainic, "Programul statului etnocratic" [The Program of the Ethnocratic State], in *Ortodoxie și etnocratie* [Orthodoxy and Ethnocracy] (Bucharest: Cugetarea, 1938), 283–84, 310–11; trans. James P. Niessen in Sugar, *Eastern European Nationalism*, 275.

enforced by the state.[36] His dream became reality in the period of the National Legionary State (*Statul Național Legionar*)—a political regime in Romania from 1940 to 1941, when the Iron Guard was the only allowed political party. Under this regime, specially appointed commissars of Romanianization carried out anti-Semitic policies adopted by the Romanian state. Officially, 450 persons were maltreated in this period, including nine assassinations. A common practice was pressing owners of businesses, sometimes by torture, to sign ownership over to Romanians. Often the beneficiaries of such relocation of property were legionnaires, and most maltreatments affected Jews.[37] According to some reports, even Orthodox priests benefited from Jewish property. For instance, Romanian gendarmerie reported that in 1941 a priest "took over through the use of terror the business of a Jew, forcing him to cede the property and to sign a contract certifying that."[38]

Abuses against Jews were a result of the nationalistic ideology of *Românianism*, which blamed Jews for the poverty and misfortunes of the Romanian population. The top church hierarchy articulated this ideology; for

36. Mihail Polihroniade, "National-socialismul și problema jidoveasca" [National Socialism and the Jewish Question], *Buna Vestire*, February 11, 1938.

37. See Vladimir Solonari, *Purifying the Nation: Population Exchange and Ethnic Cleansing in Nazi-Allied Romania* (Baltimore, MD: Johns Hopkins University Press, 2010), 129–30.

38. In Popa, *Romanian Orthodox Church*, 49.

instance, Patriarch Miron Cristea called Jews parasites in the body of the Romanian people:

> One has to be sorry for the poor Romanian people, whose very marrow is sucked out by the Jews. Not to react against the Jews means that we go open-eyed to our destruction. . . . To defend ourselves is a national and patriotic duty. This is not "antisemitism." Where is it written that only you, the Jews, have the privilege of living on some other people's back and on our back, like some parasites? You have sufficient qualities and opportunities to look for, find and acquire a country, a homeland that is not yet inhabited by others. . . . Live, help each other, defend yourselves, and exploit one another, but not us and other peoples whose entire wealth you are taking away with your ethnic and Talmudic sophistications.[39]

The anti-Semitic rhetoric of Miron's successor, Patriarch Nicodim Munteanu, was also eloquent. Nicodim presented Jews as soldiers of the Communist "Satan":

> The Bolshevik dragon spread poison upon us from outside the country. And inside he found wretched souls who became his mercenaries. Let us praise God that these Satan's soldiers were found mostly among the sons of the foreigners, the ones that called upon themselves and upon their children the curse, since they hanged on the Cross the Son of God, the Redeemer of our souls.[40]

---

39. In Popa, *Romanian Orthodox Church*, 27.

In addition to religious demagogy in depicting Jews, there were attempts to substantiate anti-Semitism theologically. Thus, Nichifor Crainic, a professor of theology in Bucharest and Chisinau, argued that Jesus Christ was not a Jew, and genuine Christianity had nothing to do with Judaism. According to Crainic, Judaism persistently combats the Christian Gospel.[41] The prototypes of this sort of theological anti-Semitism can be found in German biblical criticism. Critical theories about the historical Jesus and about discontinuities in the transmission of Jesus's message to later generations of Christians were used by anti-Semites to deconstruct the Jewish underpinnings of Christianity. One of the founders of biblical criticism, Bruno Bauer (1809–1882), a fervent anti-Semite, wrote in his essay "The Jewish Question" (1843), "The hostility of the Christian world towards the Jews is . . . quite understandable. . . . Neither of the two parties can acknowledge the other and allow it to remain in existence. The existence of the one excludes the existence of the other; each one believes itself to be the representative of absolute truth."[42]

Another representative of biblical criticism, Ernest Renan (1823–1892), connected the historical Jesus with the notion of race.[43] In his *Life of Jesus*, Renan presented

40. In Popa, *Romanian Orthodox Church*, 44.
41. See Cristian Romocea, *Church and State: Religious Nationalism and State Identification in Post-Communist Romania* (London: Continuum, 2011), 135.
42. Bruno Bauer, "Die Judenfrage" [The Jewish Question], in Mendes-Flohr and Reinharz, *Jew in the Modern World*, 298.

Christ not as God but as a man who struggled with his Jewishness and eventually overcame it. This, according to Renan, made him a great personality. This story of Jesus stems from Renan's more general view on Semitism as opposed to Aryanism. He regarded the former inferior to the latter and traced the roots of Christianity to the Aryan race. In this, he was on the same page with Arthur de Gobineau (1816–1882), who was a source for Nazi racial theories[44] and who even accused Renan of plagiarism.

Distilling Christ from his Jewishness became a major task for Nazi academia. The Institute for the Study and Eradication of Jewish Influence on German Church Life (Institut zur Erforschung und Beseitigung des jüdischen Einflusses auf das deutsche kirchliche Leben) was established for this goal in 1939. It attracted many scholars from leading German universities. Its academic director, Walter Grundmann (1906–1976), was appointed professor of New Testament at the University of Jena. The task of the scholars at the Institute was to prove that Jesus was an Aryan murdered by Jews and that his anti-Jewish struggle was distorted by posterior interpreters, such as Paul.[45] Grundmann believed that the work of his colleagues continued the Reformation. Just as in the sixteenth century Christianity liberated

43. See Susannah Heschel, *The Aryan Jesus: Christian Theologians and the Bible in Nazi Germany* (Princeton: Princeton University Press, 2010), 33–38.

44. See Arthur de Gobineau, *Essai sur l'inégalité des races humaines* [Essays on the Inequality of the Human Races] (Paris: Firmin Didot, 1853).

45. Heschel, *Aryan Jesus*, 8.

itself from papism, in the twentieth century, it would liberate itself from Judaism.[46]

While the Nazis crafted a German Christ who was not Jewish, the Russians concentrated on the presumably Jewish antichrist. According to the widespread belief among the Orthodox, the antichrist will appear before the second coming of Jesus. He will imitate Jesus in offering solutions to human problems and demonstrating miracles, but his purpose will be to distract as many people as possible from Jesus. In the Russian theology underpinning anti-Semitism, the figure of the antichrist often occupies more important a place than the figure of Christ. In this theology, Jews are the most devoted epigones of the antichrist. Their purpose is to destroy the Orthodox tsardom and to establish the kingdom of their master, the antichrist. Exactly in this eschatological context of anticipation of the antichrist, Sergei Nilus published the *Protocols of the Elders of Zion* as an appendix to his book, *Antichrist as an Imminent Political Possibility*.[47] This theology, in which the figure

46. Walter Grundmann, *Die Entjudung des religiösen Lebens als Aufgabe deutscher Theologie und Kirche* [The Deificiation of Religious Life as the Task of German Theology and Church] (Weimar: Verlag Deutsche Christen, 1939), 9–10.
47. Michael Kellogg believes that this connection between anti-Semitism and the figure of antichrist in the Russian Orthodox public goes back to Vladimir Solovyov (1853–1900) and his *Three Conversations* (Kellogg, *Russian Roots of Nazism*, 58). This is probably an exaggeration, as the standpoints of Nilus and Solovyov regarding the Jewish question were completely different. In his treatise *The Jewish Question,* Solovyov argues that while Jews always had a Jewish attitude to Christianity, Christians never had a Christian attitude to Judaism. His own attitude demonstrated a lot of sympathy and compassion with the Jewish people. Nilus's anti-Jewish eschatology

of the antichrist seems to be even more important than the figure of Christ, is probably one of the most radical forms of unorthodox Orthodoxy. The core of the Christian faith, the person of Jesus Christ, is replaced here by his antipode. Anti-Semitism makes this substitution possible.

The Soviet state made atheism its official ideology. It also officially denounced any sort of nationalism, including anti-Semitism. Unofficially, however, anti-Semitism resurfaced in Russia under Iosif Stalin, who launched a campaign of exterminating the so-called "cosmopolitans," meaning Jews. Consequent Soviet leaders also unofficially endorsed anti-Semitism. For example, all Soviet citizens were equal according to the Constitution. However, in reality Jews had fewer chances to get a good job or be promoted. They were also impeded from emigrating to Israel. In retaliation of these policies, the United States Congress in 1974 passed the Jackson-Vanik amendment to the Trade Act of 1974, which imposed economic sanctions on the Soviet Union.

After the collapse of the Soviet atheist state, religion came back from the ghetto. This has been called a "spiritual renaissance" (духовное возрождение), and it was marked by the restoration and building of new

instead is closer to Dostoyevsky's, who contrasted the Russian people as the "bearer of God" to the Jews as "bearers of antichrist" (Letter 878 to Y. Abaza, June 15, 1880, in *Polnoye sobraniye sochineniy* [Complete Collection of Works], 30:191.

churches, mass baptisms, and an increase in the number of churchgoers. Spiritual and theological literature was unbanned and filled bookshelves in bookstores and homes. Resurgence of anti-Semitism became a part of the spiritual renaissance.[48] Old anti-Semitic books from the period before the Bolshevik revolution were reprinted, and new anti-Semitic books were composed. Books by Sergei Nilus became bestsellers again, alongside collections such as *Russia before the Second Coming.* This work was published by the largest Russian monastery—the Lavra of St. Sergiy—in 1993, soon after the end of the Soviet Union.[49] It is full of quotes and "prophecies," often falsified or originating from unconfirmed sources, about the imminent coming of the antichrist. Among other forgeries and anti-Semitic passages, it included the *Protocols of the Elders of Zion.*

An even more anti-Semitic anthology, *The Mystery of Lawlessness in the Historical Ways of Russia,* was published more recently, in 2002.[50] It includes two anti-

48. See Carol Garrard and John Garrard, *Russian Orthodoxy Resurgent* (Princeton: Princeton University Press, 2009), 127; Viktor Shnirelman, "Eskhatologiya, prorochestva o kontse sveta i antisemitizm v postsovyetskoy Rossii" [Eschatology, Prophecies about the End of the World and Anti-Semitism in Post-Soviet Russia], *Forum noveyshey vostochnoyevropeyskoy istorii i kultury* [Forum of the Newest Eastern-European History and Culture] 1 (2015): 293–324.

49. Sergey Fomin, *Rossiya pered vtorym prishestviyem* [Russia before the Second Coming] (Moscow: Holy Trinity and St. Sergius Lavra, 1993). In the period 1993–2005, around two hundred thousand copies of the book were sold; see 306.

50. Y. K. Begunov, A. D. Stepanov, K. Y. Dushenov, *Tayna bezzakoniya v istoricheskikh sud'bakh Rossii* [The Mystery of Lawlessness in the Historical Ways of Russia] (St. Petersburg: Tsarskoye Delo, 2002).

Semitic articles by Metropolitan Ioann Snychev of St. Petersburg (1927–1995).[51] As the third hierarch in the ranks of the Russian Orthodox Church (after the patriarch and the metropolitan of Kyiv), he was also a leader of the group of activists whose members were both monarchists and anti-Semites. Although most hierarchs, including Patriarch Aleksiy II (1929–2008), did not share the views of Metropolitan Ioann, they allowed him to disseminate anti-Semitic propaganda on behalf of the Russian Orthodox Church. More recently the issue of anti-Semitism resurfaced on the official level in connection with the remnants of the Romanov family, which were found in the place of their execution by Bolsheviks. An influential figure in the Russian Orthodox hierarchy with close ties to the Kremlin, Bishop Tikhon Shevkunov addressed this issue at a press conference in November 2017. He suggested that the murder of the royal family might have been ritual. He thus alluded to the popular conspiracy theory that Jews killed the Romanovs according to Kabbalah rite, as a sacrifice to their religion. Representatives of the Russian state, who were present at the press conference, did not object to the statement of Bishop Tikhon. On the contrary, they promised to investigate whether the murder of the last tsar's family was ritual.[52] The

51. "Tayna bezzakoniya" [The Mystery of Lawlessness] and "Tvortsy kataklizmov [Perpetrators of Cataclysms].
52. See the Russian Service BBC, November 28, 2017, https://tinyurl.com/ybocj2r4.

statement by Bishop Tikhon caused protests among the Jewish communities and public figures inside and outside Russia. It has demonstrated that anti-Semitism is still alive in the Russian Orthodoxy, even on the official level.

In contrast to the standpoint of Metropolitan Ioann and Bishop Tikhon, many hierarchs, theologians, and laypeople in the Orthodox church have regarded anti-Semitism as a sin. While there are many examples, probably the most remarkable example of Orthodox resistance to anti-Semitism is Maria Skobtsova (1891–1945), a Russian nun who together with the priest Dimitriy Klepinin (1904–1944) helped many Jews in Nazi-occupied Paris and died in the gas chamber of the Ravensbrück concentration camp. In Ukraine, the Orthodox priest Aleksiy Glagolev (1901–1972) saved many Jewish families from being sent to Babiy Yar. In Greece, the Archbishop of Athens Damaskinos (1891–1949) signed a letter of protest (March 23, 1943) against persecutions of local Jews. Some other hierarchs of the Greek church, such as Metropolitan of Thessaloniki Gennadios (1868–1951) and Metropolitan of Zakynthos Chrysostomos (1890–1958), made remarkable efforts to save Jews in their dioceses. Damaskinos and Gennadios offered themselves instead of Jews to be sent to concentration camps. Their offer, however, was declined by Nazis. In Romania, some hierarchs and priests also extended a helping hand to Jews. For instance, Metropolitans Nicolae Bălan

(1882–1955) and Tit Simedrea (1886-1971) protested against deportation of Jews during WWII. They did so in spite of their anti-Semitic views, which they had expressed earlier.[53] There were also more sincere helpers among the Romanian clergy, such as priests Toma Chircuță and Paul Teodorescu. Father Gala Galaction spoke publicly against anti-Semitism, and Fr. Gheorghe Petre was even recognized as "Righteous among the Nations" for saving Jews in Transnistria.

Anti-Semitism has many faces. In Russia and Romania, it was more mystical, while in Germany, more rationalist. It became an intrinsic part of civil and political religions in Russia, Romania, Germany, and other countries. Dostoyevsky, Iorga, Fichte, and Wagner, to name a few intellectuals, included it in the national civil religions to which they contributed. It turned, however, into a violent political religion in the cases of the Black Hundred in Russia, the Iron Guard in Romania, and the National Socialist German Workers' Party (NSDAP) in Germany. While Romanian anti-Semites, such as Nichifor Crainic, in tune with their German confederates tried to substitute Jesus's Jewishness with Romanianism or Aryanism, Russian anti-Semites effectively substituted Christ with antichrist. In all above-mentioned cases, anti-Semitism was regarded as a part of Christian Orthodoxy. In effect, however, it is an unorthodox Orthodoxy that goes

---

53. Metropolitan Nicolae openly expressed anti-Semitic views. See Popa, *Romanian Orthodox Church*, 34, 57.

against core Christian beliefs. It targets the personality of Jesus Christ by trying to strip him of his real humanity or substituting him with the figure of antichrist. In both cases, it corresponds to the classical Orthodox criteria of heresy.

5

———

Case Study: Nationalism

Many Orthodox churches uphold different forms of political Orthodoxy. Yet there is a form of it common for most churches—nationalism. Nationalism is one of the most powerful political devices that can unite masses of people. It is capable of creating a feeling of belonging and destiny for millions. Those millions, driven by nationalism, can act together as one person, sometimes being led by one person. Nationalism is a controversial device because its basic function is to separate "us" from "them." "We," being moved by nationalist sentiment, feel ourselves superior to "them." This feeling of superiority differentiates nationalism from patriotism. Patriotism makes "us" appreciate our togetherness as a nation and, at the same time, inspires "us" to respect other nations. Nationalism makes "us" think of ourselves as superior and despise other nations as inferior. Then "we" come to hate our neighbors, and sometimes even to kill "them."

Nationalism is powerful enough to build walls between nations and at the same time to pull down some high and thick walls within the same nation. For instance, it can demolish the wall between social classes of people when they discover that they belong to the same nation. A wall, which is of particular concern for the church, has been erected by secularism. It separates the church from the public square and political arena, where it had dominated before modernity purged them. For many Orthodox churches, nationalism has become a ticket to re-enter the secularized public and political space. Because nationalism is a card played by many political parties in the Orthodox nations, the churches also play this card to remain a part of the political process. Moreover, nationalism for many Orthodox peoples is not only a political program but also a system of beliefs, where nation is worshiped like a deity. The churches, which know how to worship better than politicians, often play the nationalist card more convincingly than politicians do. The churches have to pay a price for that, however—by allowing themselves to be politicized. The churches that entertain nationalist sentiment sooner or later embark on a form of political Orthodoxy.

There are two main theories of nationalism. According to one, nationalism is an exclusive product of the era of modernity. One of the earliest students of nationalism, Elie Kedourie (1926–1992), credited Immanuel Kant (1724–1804) and the Enlightenment for its emergence.[1] Eric Hobsbawm (1914–2012) connected the idea of nationalism with the emergence of capitalism.[2] In his book *Nations and Nationalism since 1780*, he traced the roots of nationalism back to the French revolution.[3] Benedict Anderson (1936–2015) pushed the origins of nationalism a bit earlier, to the print revolution and the process of substitution of Latin with vernacular languages in Europe.[4] Ernest Gellner (1925–1995) suggested that modern nations never really existed but were *invented* in the modern era.[5] From the perspective of this theory, nationalism and ideology are homogenous—both are products of modernity. Moreover, nationalism is probably the most powerful and long-lasting version of ideology.[6]

1. See Adrian Hastings, *The Construction of Nationhood: Ethnicity, Religion, and Nationalism* (Cambridge: Cambridge University Press, 1997), 10.
2. See Hastings, *Contruction of Nationhood*, 10.
3. Eric J. Hobsbawm, *Nations and Nationalism since 1780: Programme, Myth, Reality*, (Cambridge: Cambridge University Press, 1990).
4. See Benedict Anderson, *Imagined Communities: Reflections on the Origin and Spread of Nationalism* (London: Verso, 2006), 39.
5. Ernest Gellner, *Thought and Change* (Chicago: University of Chicago Press, 1965), 168.

Indeed, national identity has the same ideocratic nature as any ideology—the differentiation between ethnic groups is defined, in Benedict Anderson's words, only "by the style in which they are imagined."[7]

The term *nation* in the modern sense was introduced to political discourse by Jean-Jacques Rousseau, who also coined other terms pertinent to modernity, such as *social contract* and *civil religion*. In the "Plan for a Constitution for Corsica" (*Projet de constitution pour la Corse*, 1765), he stated, "Every people has or ought to have a national character, and if it lack one it would be necessary to begin by giving it one."[8] Although the idea of nation was first articulated by a devoted secularist, it soon became appropriated by Christian churches. The French abbé Emmanuel Joseph Sieyès (1748–1836) rendered the concept of nation in metaphysical terms: "The nation exists before everything, it is the object of everything. Its will is always legal, it is the law itself."[9] This is effectively a profession of the civil religion close to the Orthodox version of it, with nation occupying the place of deity in its temple.

---

6. John Breuilly has called it "the most important political ideology of the modern era." John Breuilly, "Reflections on Nationalism," in Stuart Woolf, ed., *Nationalism in Europe, 1815 to the Present: A Reader* (London: Routledge, 1996), 137.

7. Anderson, *Imagined Communities,* 6.

8. Jean-Jacques Rousseau, *The Plan for Perpetual Peace, on the Government of Poland, and other Writings on History and Politics* (Lebanon, NH: University Press of New England, 2011), 133.

9. Murray Greensmith Forsyth, *Reason and Revolution: The Political Thought of the Abbé Sieyes* (Leicester: Leicester University Press, 1987), 76.

Rousseau's concept of nation is intrinsically connected with his other idea of social contract. The social contract, as he envisaged it, shifted political authority from monarchs to people. This process, however, ruptured the cohesion of a people. The concept of nation was supposed to restore fractured social cohesion. People now could be united not as subjects of a king but as a nation. In consolidating around their elected representatives, who exercised political authority not by God's will but by the will of citizens, citizens were supposed to act as a nation. Nation became a source of legitimacy for representative republican governments and a common political space to which all people belonged regardless of their birth, wealth, and religion.[10] Civil religion, as envisaged by Rousseau, also provided a common space for all citizens, restored social cohesion, and legitimized republican governments. All modern republics have incorporated to different degrees the Rousseauian concepts of social contract and nations as devices enhancing the cohesion of people.

An alternative theory of nationalism claims that national identity stems from early human civilizations.[11] Hugh Seton-Watson, Doron Mendels, and Susan Reynolds argue that the roots of some modern nations

---

10. See Erica Benner, "Nationalism: Intellectual Origins," in John Breuilly, ed., *The Oxford Handbook of the History of Nationalism* (Oxford: Oxford University Press, 2013), 39.
11. See Peter Burke, "Nationalism and Vernaculars, 1500–1800," in Benner, "Nationalism," 21.

go back deep to the premodern past.[12] These roots are well distinguished during the Middle Ages. Some medieval European nations emerged from the patronage of particular saints: England with St. Georges and Spain with St. James. Medieval political propaganda emphasized a distinct character of some nations on the basis of their religious mission: "most Christian kingdom" of France, "Catholic monarchy" of Spain, and so on.

There is apparently not much contradiction between modern and premodern theories of nationalism. On the one hand, a nation in the modern sense is a device shaped in the frame of modernity. This device cannot be exactly identified in the premodern era. On the other hand, protonations are identifiable as early as classical antiquity. For instance, one can interpret the following definition of the Greeks by Herodotus (c. 484–c. 425 BCE) as prototypical for most modern national identities: "There is the Greek nation [τὸ Ἑλληνικόν]—the community of blood and language, temples and ritual, and our common customs."[13]

Although there is a continuity between premodern protonations and modern nations, there is also a fun-

---

12. Hugh Seton-Watson, *Nations and States: An Enquiry into the Origins of Nations and the Politics of Nationalism* (Boulder, CO: Westview, 1977); Doron Mendels, *Memory in Jewish, Pagan, and Christian Societies of the Graeco-Roman World* (London: T&T Clark, 2004); Susan Reynolds, *Kingdoms and Communities in Western Europe, 900–1300* (Oxford: Oxford University Press, 1984).
13. Herodotus, *Histories*, 8.144.1–3, trans. Aubrey de Sélincourt (London: Penguin, 2003).

damental difference between them: modern nationalism belongs completely to the secular frame, while premodern protonationalisms transcended this frame and featured metaphysical references. In particular, many protonationalisms were built on the idea of being chosen by God. Thus, Girolamo Savonarola (1452–1498) enchanted the Florentines with the idea that they were an elect nation. The Reformation developed this idea further by bestowing upon some "chosen nations" a mission to reform Christianity. As a result, German Lutheran, English Anglican, Scottish Presbyterian, Dutch Reformed, and American Puritan exceptionalisms contributed to the formation of corresponding nations. Eastern protonationalisms also featured the idea of religious election. However, in contrast to the Western mission to reform Christianity, they considered their mission to be preserving Christianity in its traditional forms. This idea especially drove Greek, Romanian, Russian, and some other nationalisms inspired by the idea of preserving Byzantium in modernity.

Probably the earliest forms of protonationalism in the Christian East were doctrinal, when a theological movement transformed a people's identity. Such was Arianism. As explained earlier, it was a theological doctrine articulated in the fourth century by the Alexandrian presbyter Arius. Arius taught that Jesus Christ is not God but the creature of the Father and introduced hierarchy into the Trinity. Roman emperors, who liked the idea of hierarchy, extended their support for this doctrine, which became Orthodoxy for the majority of the Christian communities in the East in the middle of the fourth century. Approximately at this time the nomadic Goths received Christianity in its Arian form. Toward the end of the century, the imperial church got rid of Arianism, which was rebuked as heresy. Goths, however, preserved it, not so much as a theological doctrine but as a protonational identity. The translation of the Bible into Gothic by the Arian bishop Wulfila (c. 311–383) contributed to the transformation of the doctrinal affiliation of the Goths into their protonational identity.

Even more lasting protonational identities were shaped by the theological controversies regarding the person and natures of Jesus Christ. In the beginning of the fifth century, a group of eastern Syrians adopted a teaching articulated by Theodoros of Mopsuestia (c. 350–c. 428) and promoted by the patriarch of Constantinople Nestorios (c. 386–c. 450). This teaching, also known as Nestorianism, stressed the humanity of Jesus Christ and, many believed, introduced a distinct human subject to his personality. It was condemned by the Third Ecumenical Council of Ephesos (431). As a result, many Nestorians fled to Persia. In the Persian empire, the Nestorian doctrine gradually became a protonational identity of what is now known as the Assyrian people.[14]

Soon after the Council of Ephesos, the Council of Chalcedon (451) decided that all Christians in the Roman empire should recognize Christ as having two natures, not one. However, many Egyptians and western Syrians disagreed with this decision. They formed confessional groups that adopted the names of the leaders of dissent: Theodosians after the name of the Alexandrian Patriarch Theodosios (d. 567), Severans after the Patriarch of Antioch Severos (465–538), and Jacobites after the bishop of Edessa Jacob Baradaeus (d. 578). These groups built their identities on the rejection of the Council of Chalcedon. These religious identities gradually developed into ethnic ones: Copts, Syrians, and Armenians.[15] Their common denominator became their rejection of (1) the Greek language, (2) Roman rule, and (3) Chalcedonian Orthodoxy.

In contrast, these three features were reaffirmed in Byzantium, where they eventually evolved into the Byzantine protonational identity.[16] This identity is called "Byzantine" by mistake—in reality it was "Roman" identity. The "Byzantines" did not call themselves Byzantines, but Romans. They identified

14. See Cyril Hovorun, *From Antioch to Xi'an: An Evolution of "Nestorianism"* (Hong Kong: Chinese Orthodox Press, 2014).
15. Armenian national identity has become particularly strong. In Pew research, it is on the top of the list of national identities connected with religion—82 percent (Pew Research Center, "Religious Belief and National Belonging in Central and Eastern Europe," *Pew Reserach Center*, May 10, 2017, PDF, 12, available for download: https://tinyurl.com/ldtj6at.
16. See George Ostrogorsky, *History of the Byzantine State* (New Brunswick, NJ: Rutgers University Press, 1969), 27.

themselves with the Roman empire, spoke the Greek language, and believed that the theology articulated by the seven Ecumenical Councils is the only true version of Christianity. This identity, which became known as Ρωμηοσύνη, or *Romanitas*, had political, religious, and cultural components.[17] Some of these components survived the collapse of the Eastern Roman empire, which had given the Roman identity its name.

Roman identity was modified in the Muslim Ottoman empire, which succeeded Byzantium. There, non-Muslim religious minorities were organized into politically semi-autonomous groups called *millets*. Roman identity evolved further within the "Roman" *millet* (*millet-i Rûm*), which comprised all Orthodox Christians of the Ottoman state. This *millet* became a protonation from which modern nations of Greeks, Serbs, Montenegrins, Bulgars, Albanians, Romanians, and other Orthodox peoples in the Balkans sprang later on in the nineteenth century. The organizational principle of *millets* was religious: *Yahud milleti* included all Jews; *millet-i Ermeniyan,* all non-Chalcedonians; *millet-i Rûm,* all Chalcedonians; and the latest, *Katolik millet*, provided autonomy for all Roman Catholics. Each *millet* had its own taxation, education, and courts. Their top hierarchs were also political leaders for their flocks. For instance, the political leader of the Roman

17. See Claudia Rapp, "Hellenic Identity, *Romanitas*, and Christianity in Byzantium," in *Hellenisms: Culture, Identity, and Ethnicity from Antiquity to Modernity*, ed. Katerina Zacharia (Aldershot: Ashgate, 2008), 127–47.

millet was the patriarch of Constantinople, who had the title *millet-başı*.

The Ottoman *millet* system culminated in the nineteenth century during the *Tanzimât* reforms, which tried to accommodate increasing demands of religious minorities. The reforms triggered a gradual transformation of *millets* from a system based on religious identity to an ethnic system. Some ethnic groups from these *millets*, emancipated from the Ottoman empire through revolutions and wars, established their own national states. Among them were Greeks, Romanians, Bulgars, Serbs, and Montenegrins from the *millet-i Rûm*. Other peoples—such as Copts, Syrians, and Armenians, who belonged to the "Armenian" *millet* (*millet-i Ermeniyan*)—did not gain statehood for themselves. For the Armenians, their national rise ended tragically with the genocide of 1915–1917, when Turkish authorities exterminated around 1.5 million Armenians. The first modern Armenian state was founded only in 1918 on the territory of the Russian empire, which just had collapsed. However, it was soon absorbed in the Soviet Union. The Habsburg Empire faced the same desire for emancipation from its ethnic minorities. Serbs, Romanians, Ukrainians, and Ruthenians looked for their own states independent from Austro-Hungary.

All of these emancipatory movements in the empires where Eastern Christians constituted religious minorities were driven by national ideology, which evolved to the Balkan-style ethnic nationalism. This style of nationalism was "derivative," in the words of Peter van der Veer.[18] It had been born in the context of the Western Enlightenment and then transmitted to an Eastern context. Western ideas about nation were disseminated through philhellenes like Lord Byron (1788–1824), who projected his English nationalism onto Greece,[19] or through Orthodox intellectuals in the diaspora, such as Adamantios Koraïs (1748–1833). These intellectuals learned new ideas about nation from books and discussions in the Western salons and then brought them to their homelands.

Koraïs, for instance, borrowed his concept of Greek nation from the discussions at the "Society of Observers of Man" (*Société des observateurs de l'homme*). There Koraïs, the only foreign member of the society, called for Greek antiquity to be the foundation of the new Greek nation.[20] He explained his plan for the renewal of the Greek nation using the language of commerce. According to him, when Europe was emerging from barbarianism, it borrowed intellectual treasures from the ancient Greeks. Now it was time for Europe to pay the debt.[21] Koraïs coined a word for this business: *Metakinosis* (Μεταχίνωσις), which can be translated as

18. Peter van der Veer, "Nationalism and Religion," in Breuilly, *Oxford Handbook of the History of Nationalism*, 655.
19. See Maria Koundoura, *The Greek Idea: The Formation of National and Transnational Identities* (London: Tauris, 2007), 64.
20. See Olga Augustinos, "Philhellenic Promises and Hellenic Visions: Korais and the Discourses of the Enlightenment," in Zacharia, *Hellenisms*, 169.
21. See Augustinos, "Philhellenic Promises," 191.

"transmission." He dreamed of *Metakinosis* as a transplantation of European education and intellectual culture to Greek soil. In terms of the theories of nationalism, Koraïs belonged to the premodern school, as he traced the Greek nation to antiquity. Since then, in his opinion, Greek national culture only declined: first under the Romans, then in the Byzantine period, and eventually falling to lethargy under the Ottomans. For Koraïs, only returning to the "golden age" of the Athenian democracy could raise the Greek nation from ashes.

In addition to French ideas, there was significant German input in the formation of nationalism in the Balkan countries. Germany's advanced classical studies were among the key factors that ignited European philhellenism in the beginning of the nineteenth century.[22] German idealism inspired intellectuals in Orthodox countries to idealize nationhood. The German concept of language as an instrument of national formation became particularly important in the Balkans. Because Germany was politically divided during most of the nineteenth century, it could not offer to all Germans a common social contract like the French. Instead, Johann Gottfried von Herder (1744–1803) suggested consolidating the German people on the ground of common language. Johann Gottlieb Fichte interpreted language as culture in a broad sense. He

22. See Glenn Most, "Philhellenism, Cosmopolitanism, Nationalism," in Zacharia, *Hellenisms*, 151.

suggested that cultural sovereignty could be even stronger than political sovereignty and must be developed by any group of people that seeks to be called a nation.[23]

In line with German ideas, Orthodox minorities in both the Ottoman and Habsburg empires began their national struggle by defining themselves culturally. People's vernacular was standardized, and literature was produced in spoken Greek, Bulgarian, Serbian, and other languages. Campaigns were launched to establish networks of national schools, which were to become nurseries for language and culture. Soon, however, the new nations began arguing about whose culture was superior. That is how emancipatory national identities turned to nationalisms. Nationalism, in turn, led emerging Orthodox nations to wage wars against one another.

During the first stage of the so-called Balkan wars (1912–13), Orthodox Greeks, Bulgars, Serbs, and Montenegrins fought together against Turks. That was still an emancipatory phase of the formation of Orthodox national identities. At the second stage of the Balkan wars, however, Bulgaria launched a military campaign against Greece and Serbia, while Romania invaded Bulgaria. This was a phase when ethnic identity transformed to nationalism. Nationalism challenged the sol-

---

23. See Erica Benner, "Nationalism: Intellectual Origins," in Breuilly, *Oxford Handbook of the History of Nationalism*, 45–46.

idarity of the Orthodox nations and reversed their initial liberation momentum.

French and German modes of nationalism began competing with each other among the ethnic minorities in the Ottoman and Habsburg empires. The difference between these two modes is sometimes identified as German *jus sangunis*—the right of blood—versus the French *jus soli*—the right of land.[24] That is, being French required living on French land while being German meant being born German by blood, regardless of where this happened. France, in the period of the formation of national ideas, was a strong unitarian state, while during its national development, Germany was an agglomerate of independent polities. The Orthodox minorities in the Ottoman and Habsburg empires were in a situation similar to Germany's—they did not have their own state. In addition, they shared their land with a Muslim majority, whom they did not want to include in their nations. As a result, they eventually embraced nationalism based on blood, not on soil, even though initially they had been inspired by the French idea of nation.

John Breuilly has defined nationalism as "a politics that seeks autonomy for the nation."[25] This definition fully applies to Eastern Christian nationalisms. The

---

24. See Rogers Brubaker, *Citizenship and Nationhood in France and Germany* (Cambridge, MA: Harvard University Press, 1992).
25. John Breuilly, "Nationalism and National Unification in Nineteenth-Century Europe," in Breuilly, *Oxford Handbook of the History of Nationalism*, 150.

efforts of the minorities that emerged from the two empires to define themselves through religion, culture, and education eventually led to their struggle for political independence. Independence became a categorical imperative for all Orthodox nationalist movements. German idealism was inspirational once again. Hegel, while dealing with nationalism in his own context, envisioned a unified German national state (*Nationalstaat*) with strong political authority and a powerful army. For him, an accomplished nation meant a nation protected by the independent state. Only the people (*Völker*) whose national states had meaningful and dignified existence deserved to be active *subjects* of the historical process and not just its passive *objects*.[26]

While national awakening in the West was rather secular, in the East it had a strong religious dimension. Notably, the Orthodox church played a more important role in national awakening in the territories of the Ottoman empire and was less active in the Habsburg dominion. Serbian nation-building, for instance, consisted of two components: an ecclesial component generated in Belgrade (in Ottoman territory), and a cultural one, which originated from Vojvodina, part of the Habsburg state. Romanian nation-building developed similarly: its cultural component came from Habsburg Transylvania, while its ecclesial platform was in

26. See Armin von Bogdandy, "Hegel und der Nationalstaat," *Der Staat* 30, no. 4 (1991): 513–35.

Wallachia and Moldavia—two autonomous principalities under Ottoman control.

The influence of the churches on the formation of national statehood was not unilateral: national statehood affected the churches in return. For instance, during the period of national struggles it became commonly understood that the Orthodox nations should have their own autocephalous churches. Autocephaly in the nineteenth century became a form of what Peter van der Veer calls "nationalization of religion."[27] It turned into a synonym for national sovereignty and became a necessary attribute of an accomplished nation, along with language, culture, and an educational system. Only an Orthodox nation with its own autocephalous church was considered dignified and a subject, not object of the historical process, to put it in Hegelian terms. The first instance of this type of autocephaly was the Greek church, which unilaterally proclaimed its independence from the church of Constantinople in 1833. Even so, the independence of the Greek church was not recognized by the church of Constantinople until 1850. It took even longer to recognize the Bulgarian church, which proclaimed its independence in 1872 but was only accepted by Constantinople in 1945.

The procedure of declaring autocephaly based on national identity was different than the autocephaly

27. Van der Veer, "Nationalism and Religion," in Breuilly, *Oxford Handbook of the History of Nationalism*, 657.

process in late antiquity and the Middle Ages. In earlier times, autocephaly was negotiated, often by political figures, and proclaimed as a result of agreements between imperial and ecclesial authorities.[28] In the nineteenth century, the procedure followed the pattern of the proclamation of independent states. These states proclaimed their independence unilaterally, without consulting the empires they wanted to leave. Of course, empires in most cases did not recognize the new states, which thus existed for a long time without full recognition. The same applied to autocephalies, which were first proclaimed unilaterally, and only afterwards came to be recognized by their mother church.

The process through which independent Orthodox nations obtained autocephaly for their churches had a tremendous impact on these churches. On the one hand, they confirmed themselves as popular institutions standing by their people. On the other hand, many local Orthodox churches evolved into "parcels of national identity," in the words of van der Veer.[29] Orthodoxy was sublimated to ethnic identity. As a result, even now people who identify themselves as

---

28. See Cyril Hovorun, "Autocephaly as a Diachronic Phenomenon and Its Ukrainian Case," in *A Jubilee Collection: Essays in Honor of Professor Paul Robert Magocsi*, ed. Valerii Padiak and Patricia Krafcik (Uzhhorod: Valerii Padiak, 2015), 273–80.

29. van der Veer, "Nationalism and Religion," in Breuilly, *Oxford Handbook of the History of Nationalism*, 658.

Orthodox conflate their Orthodox identity with being a Serb, a Bulgarian, or a Russian, for example.

While Greek, Bulgarian, Serbian, Romanian, and other Balkan nationalisms are particularist and aim at building a single nation, there is another sort of nationalism that goes beyond only one nation. It can be called *civilizational*. The subject of this nationalism is not a nation, but a civilization.[30] Civilization is larger and less particularist than nationhood. Lev Gumilyov (1912–1992) called civilization a "super-ethnos."[31] Such super-nations are "fixed organisms" driven by their own values and logic.[32] Each of them acts according to its own understanding of its place in history. In this regard, civilizations, like nations, interpret themselves in Hegelian terms but believe themselves to be more powerful subjects of history than nations.

The concept of civilization became extremely popular in the Orthodox milieu. There are two major Orthodox editions of civilizational nationalism: Greek and Russian. Both echo the ideas of Victor de Riqueti,

---

30. The concept of civilization was developed in the twentieth century by Arnold Toynbee (1889–1975), Quincy Wright (1890–1970), and others. It had earlier precedents in the works of Oswald Spengler (1880–1936), who used the word *cultures* for "civilizations." See Oswald Spengler, *Der Untergang des Abendlandes* (München: Beck, 1923); English translation: *The Decline of the West* (London: G. Allen & Unwin, 1926). See also Arnold Toynbee, *Hellenism: The History of a Civilization* (New York: Oxford University Press, 1959); Quincy Wright, *A Study of War* (Chicago: University of Chicago Press, 1983); and *The Causes of War and the Conditions of Peace* (London: Longmans, Green, 1981).

31. See Lev Gumilev, *Ethnogenesis and the Biosphere* (Moscow: Progress, 1990).

32. Bruce Mazlish, *Civilization and Its Contents* (Stanford: Stanford University Press, 2004), xii.

Marquis de Mirabeau (1715–1789), who in his treatise *L'Ami des hommes* (1756) defined religion as "the first source of civilization."[33] Mirabeau implied that civilization is both civility as opposed to barbarianism, and a geopolitical organism whose energy and identity stem from religion.[34]

Greek civilizational nationalism is built on the idea of civilization as the opposite of barbarianism. It is built on a dichotomization between "us"—civilized people—and "them"—the barbarians. This dichotomization goes back to the fifth century BCE, when Greeks waged wars against Persians. The Greeks identified Persians—"them"—as "barbarians."[35] Many modern Greek nationalists continue seeing the world in black and white—as "civilized us" against "barbarian them." According to 2017 Pew research, Greeks are on the top of the list of the Orthodox nations who consider themselves culturally superior to other nations—89 percent.[36]

Greek theologians cast this civilizational nationalism in theological terms. Father Ioannis Romanidis (1927–2001) and his disciple Fr. Georgios Metallinos (born in 1940) produced a theology of Greek civilization, which they encapsulated in the term *Romanitas*

---

33. In Mazlish, *Civilization and Its Contents*, 5.
34. He was a father of the famous activist of the French revolution Honoré Gabriel Riqueti, comte de Mirabeau (1749–1791).
35. See Katerina Zacharia, "Herodotus' Four Markers of Greek Identity," in Zacharia, *Hellenisms*, 25–27.
36. Pew Research Center, "Religious Belief and National Belonging," 13.

(Ρωμηοσύνη).[37] *Romanitas* is constituted by Orthodox faith and Eastern identity.

Greek theologians who follow this line present Hellenism as the opposite of Western barbarianism. They share the idea, first articulated by Romanidis, that the alienation of the West from Orthodoxy began with Augustine, was later embodied by Franks in the European medieval kingdoms, culminated in the crusades, and continues in Western consumerist societies. For them, Greek civilization is built on genuine Orthodox faith, while Western civilization is built on a heretical interpretation of Christianity.[38] Even in its secularized form, Western civilization continues to be heretical. Thus, it developed a distorted form of Orthodox universality (οἰκουμενικότητα)—globalization.[39]

---

37. See Andrew J. Sopko, *The Theology of John Romanides: Prophet of Roman Orthodoxy* (Dewdney, BC: Synaxis, 1998); Hierotheos Vlakhos, *P. Ioannis Romanidis—enas korifeos dogmatikos theologos tis Orthodoksu Katholikis Ekklisias* [Fr. Ioannis Romanidis—A Leading Systematic Theologian of the Orthodox Universal Church] (Nafpaktos: Monastery of the Nativity of the Virgin, 2012). See George Metallinos, *Sta monopatia tis Romiosinis* [On the Paths of Romanitas] (Athens: Armos, 2008); George Metallinos, *O Romios ke to thavma* [A Roman and the Miracle] (Athens: Armos, 2011); George Metallinos, *O Laos tu Theu: istorika ke theologika tu Romaiku Ellinismu* [The People of God: The Historical and Theological Aspects of the Roman Hellenism] (Athens: Armos, 2015).

38. See Christos Yannaras, *Orthodoksia ke Disi sti Neoteri Ellada* [Orthodoxy and the West in Modern Greece] (Athens: Domos, 2006), 56; Nikos Matsukas, *Ellinorthodoksi paradosi ke ditikos politismos* [The Greek Orthodox Tradition and Western Civilization] (Thessaloniki: Minima, 1985); Marios Begzos, *I metafisiki tis usiokratias sto Meseona ke i. Filosofiki kritiki sti thriskia tis Evropis* [The Metaphysics of Essence Dominion During the Middle Ages and Secularization: A Philosophical Critique of the European Religion] (Athens: Private edition, 1989).

The Russian version of an Orthodox civilization is the "Russian world." People who associate themselves with this world usually criticize modern Western "civilization." In contrast to the followers of Hellenism, however, they do not make references to barbarianism. Civilizations constitute centers of gravity in the world, which thus should be multipolar. Such a world is promoted as an alternative to what is described as a uni-polar world of American dominance.[40]

The "Russian world" is often presented as a distinct "Russian civilization." The main forum of the "Russian world," the World Russian People's Council, at its 2001 meeting, which was also attended by Vladimir Putin, chose as its theme "Russia: Faith and Civilization." The council concluded that Russia "is one of the pillars of the Eastern Christian world and a center of a self-sufficient civilization." This implies that world order "should be reshaped on the principles of multipolarity. . . . The modern world cannot be built on one civilizational model only."[41] The rhetoric of the council repeats the ideas of Samuel Huntington (1927–2008)

---

39. See his lecture "Greek Catholicity and Western Globalism," delivered at the Foundation Anieli, Turin, Italy, in Christos Yannaras, *I Aristera os Deksia, i Deksia os pantomima. Stikhia kritikis analisis tu neoelliniku Midenismu* [The Left as Right, the Right as Pantomime. Elements of the Critical Analysis of the Neo-Hellenic Nihilism] (Athens: Patakis, 2001), 211–30.
40. See A. G. Dugin, *Teoriya mnogopolyarnogo mira* [The Theory of the Multipolar World] (Moscow: Eurasian Renaissance, 2012).
41. *Sobornoye slovo VI Vsemirnogo Russkogo Narodnogo Sobora* [The Conciliar Word of the 6th World Russian People's Council], Moscow, December 14, 2001, https://tinyurl.com/y73gw55j.

and Alexander Panarin (1940–2003). The latter elaborated on the concept of the "Orthodox civilization."[42] According to this concept, Orthodox Christianity is the foundation of the Russian civilization.

On the one hand, civilizational nationalism is still nationalism. It claims superiority for one civilization over others, which inevitably leads to the same conflicts and tensions that are pertinent in classical nationalism. On the other hand, it is different and often even contrary to ethnic nationalism, which is based on the concept of nationhood. From the perspective of civilizational nationalism, ethnic nationalism reduces the grandeur of civilizations, which have broader horizons than nations. For example, a zealous proponent of Greek civilizational nationalism and polemicist against ethnic nationalism, Christos Yannaras, despises the small size and small interests of the modern Greek state.[43] His ideal is Byzantium. Following the line of Konstantinos Paparrigopoulos, Yannaras reserves for Byzantium a central place in the history of Hellenism. Contrary to the line of Koraïs, who

---

42. See Samuel P. Huntington, "The Clash of Civilizations?," *Foreign Affairs* 72, no. 3 (August 1993): 22–49; A. S. Panarin, *Pravoslavnaya tsivilizatsiya v globalnom mire* [The Orthodox Civilization in the Global World] (Moscow: Eksmo, 2003), 210.

43. See a critical assessment of his views in Pantelis Kalaïtzidis, "Ellinikotita ke antidikitismos sti 'Theologia tu 60'" [Hellenism and anti-Westernism in the "Theology of the 60s"] (PhD thesis, Aristotle's University of Thessaloniki, 2008); Daniel P. Payne, *The Revival of Political Hesychasm in Contemporary Orthodox Thought: The Political Hesychasm of John S. Romanides and Christos Yannaras* (Lanham, MD: Lexington, 2011).

considered Hellenism in a state of permanent decline from ancient civilization, through Byzantium, to the misery of the Ottoman rule, Yannaras sees Byzantium as an apogee of Hellenism. For him, even the Ottoman empire and modern Turkey are in some sense more heirs to Byzantium than the modern Greek state is.[44] For Yannaras, Byzantine Hellenism is the "civilization" (πολιτισμός) par excellence.

The Byzantine narrative in modern Greek political discourse often led to catastrophic consequences. One of these was the so-called "Micrasian catastrophe" (Μικρασιατική καταστροφή), when Greeks were expelled from Asia Minor, after their military forces tried to capture territories in Anatolia in 1918–1922. The Greek military assault was inspired by the "Great idea"—Μεγάλη ἰδεά, a term coined by the Greek nationalist Ioannis Kolettis (1773–1847).[45] According to this idea, the Greek state should include every territory with a significant Greek population, primarily in Asia Minor. This idea envisages Greece as a continuation of Byzantine civilization. Its main goal is to recapture Constantinople. As Ion Dragoumis (1878–1920) put it in 1909,

> The great idea is a memory which remained, burrowed deeply and nested in the soul of the Romios, from the

44. Personal exchange with Yannaras during our trip to Cappadocia together with Ecumenical Patriarch Bartholomew in 2007.
45. See Richard Clogg, *A Concise History of Greece* (Cambridge: Cambridge University Press, 1992), 48.

time that the Turks, in 1453, took the City [Constantinople]. It is the remembrance that the Romios, with the City as capital, possessed the East in bygone years, the Eastern state with many peoples, which he inherited little by little from the ancient Romans.[46]

Rooted in the Western European Romanticism of the nineteenth century,[47] the "Great idea" became a fundament for Greek dictatorships during the twentieth century. Ioannis Metaxas (ruled from 1936 to 1941) promoted his regime as a "Third Hellenic civilization," which is called to comprise every Greek land. For Metaxas, the first Hellenic civilization was embedded in the militarist societies of Macedonia and Sparta. Byzantium was a second civilization. In contrast to the Romantic nationalists of the nineteenth century, Metaxas's national program thus made references to Byzantium. These references enhanced his idea of a strong state in the spirit of Mussolini's "total state" (*lo stato totale*). Metaxas's Hellenism was also antidemocratic, which is why he chose not Athenian democracy but Macedonian and Spartan autocracies as its prototype.

To a greater extent than even the Greek world, the Russian world, as a civilizational nationalism, became violent and war-mongering. The war against Georgia

---

46. "Stratos ke alla" [Army, etc.] *Noumas*, December 27, 1909, translated by Gerasimos Augustinos in Sugar, *Eastern European Nationalism*, 164.

47. See Panayotis Kayas, *Khoris fovo ke pathos. Megali idea* [Without Fear and Pathos. Great Idea] (Athens: I. Sideris, 1980), 21.

in 2008 and Ukraine in 2014, conflicts in Transnistria and Nagorno-Karabakh, provocations on the borders with Baltic states, attempts at disrupting democracy in the United States and other Western countries, interventions in Syria—all these activities have been inspired by the ideology behind the Russian world. Not surprisingly, the rhetoric surrounding the "Russian world" does not lack references to Byzantium. One of its proponents, bishop Tikhon Shevkunov, produced a movie, *The Fall of an Empire: The Lesson of Byzantium*, where he metaphorically articulated a political program for Putin's Russia.[48] Vladimir Putin responded by adding allusions to Byzantium to his political agenda. For instance, during his visit to Mount Athos in May 2016, his protocol staged the ceremony of his reception by the Athonite monks in a way that resembled the rites at the Byzantine court. This was an appeal to nostalgia that many Orthodox worldwide feel about Byzantium. As a result, a significant number of Orthodox now see the Russian president as a successor to Byzantine basileuses. They are ready to turn a blind eye to the wars he wages and murders he commits.

Most support for Putin is demonstrated by the Russian Orthodox Church. Sometimes this church goes ahead of the state in calling for violence in the name of the Russian world. Thus, the official speaker of the

---

48. Bishop Tikhon Shevkunov, "The Fall of an Empire: The Lesson of Byzantium," YouTube video, 1:11:03, uploaded by "PravoslavieRu," November 15, 2012, https://tinyurl.com/pj7a6br.

Moscow Patriarchate at that time, Fr. Vsevolod Chaplin, was among the earliest voices urging Russian intervention in the wake of the Revolution of Dignity in Ukraine. He stated in his comment to the news agency *Interfax* on March 1, 2014:

> Back in 1995, the World Russian People's Council declared that the Russian people is a divided nation on its historical territory, which has the right to be reunited in a single state body, which is a generally accepted rule of international politics. . . . We hope that the mission of Russian soldiers to protect freedom and identity of these people and their very life will not meet fierce resistance.[49]

He added that military intervention would secure the "civilizational choice" for the Ukrainians in favor of Russia and would turn them away from aligning with the West. This statement was made before the Russian military occupied Crimea and invaded Donbas, when few believed that Russian aggression against Ukraine would be possible. Father Chaplin's statement referred to the idea of civilization, which, in his opinion, had a right to be consolidated on the basis of common values with the use of military force. This happened with the annexation of Crimea and the following war in Donbas as a result of Russian civilizational nationalism. In April 2018, Fr. Chaplin, no longer an official speaker

---

49. Published on the website of the World Russian People's Council, March 1, 2014, https://tinyurl.com/y957uf5g.

of the church, posted on his Facebook wall a call to occupy Kyiv and other parts of Ukraine. He added, "In contrast to the Americans, we are not afraid at all to destroy big cities."[50]

In conclusion, national self-awareness can be a part of civil or political religion. In the former case, it can play a positive role of liberation of a nation from the empire. However, as with any civil religion, emancipatory nation-building can easily turn to its opposite—nationalism. In such cases, it becomes an instrument of oppression rather than an instrument of protection from oppression. It then coerces those who do not share the same national sentiment or who do not belong to the same nation. Nationalism often leads to clashes and wars even between the nations that share the same religious tradition. In such cases of nationalistic wars, divisions along ethnic lines seem to be deeper than commonality of faith. In effect, nationalism can function in the capacity of faith. Nationalists then venerate their ethnic identity with religious awe, which sometimes substitutes for fear of God. Oppressive nationalism can take two forms: ethnic and civilizational. The former one serves nations, and the latter one serves empires. These two forms of nationalism share the same idea of superiority over other nations/civilizations, and at the same time they exclude each other. Nevertheless, the peoples who proclaim Ortho-

50. Facebook post on April 12, 2018, at 1:14 am, https://tinyurl.com/y8xu6xov.

dox Christianity as the foundation of their nation or civilization can easily adopt either form. In such cases, nationalism compromises Orthodoxy, and turns it unorthodox.

Concluding Assessments

In this book, we have identified and studied some forms of political Orthodoxy. They are deeply embedded on different levels within the church: they are enthusiastically upheld by lay people, preached by priests, and blessed by bishops and patriarchs. They are like "a church with no buildings or membership statistics," in the words of Michael Angrosino.[1] This "church" is foreign to the church of Christ, however. Political Orthodoxies are like parasites in the ecclesial organism: while behaving like a part of the body, they consume its nutrients and intoxicate it.

All political Orthodoxies have a causal relationship with one other in the same way that sins do. Thus, civil religion easily mutates into political religion. They

---

1. Michael Angrosino, "Civil Religion Redux," *Anthropological Quarterly* 75, no. 2 (2002): 259.

both produce nationalism, which can be ethnic or imperial. When this confusion of national and religious identities occurs, it can make Orthodox people proud of themselves and hateful toward others. Historically, for many Orthodox the despised "others" were often Jews. Modern Orthodox anti-Semitism can be interpreted as a reaction to the process of modernization: it scapegoated Jews for all negative consequences of social changes brought by industrialization and globalization—as the story of the *Protocols of the Elders of Zion* shows.[2]

The *Declaration of the Council of the Orthodox Patriotic People,* penned by Fr. Vsevolod Chaplin and Viktor Aksyuchits, exemplifies the connection between various political Orthodoxies.[3] This document is in the first place a manifesto of Orthodox conservatism, which simultaneously propagates Russian nationalism. Father Chaplin, formerly an active participant in ecumenical fora on behalf of the Russian Orthodox Church, converted to rigid anti-ecumenism. This also coincided with his conversion to antimodernism and decision to support the war in Ukraine. Igor Druz', an active participant in the Ukrainian war on the Russian side, also signed the *Declaration.* He has also positioned

---

2. See Herbert Arthur Strauss, ed., *Hostages of Modernisation: Studies on Modern Antisemitism 1870-1933/39* (Berlin: de Gruyter, 1993).

3. "Deklaratsiya Sovieta pravoslavnoy patrioticheskoy obschestvennosti," adopted at the conference of the Council of the Orthodox Patriotic People in Moscow on April 18, 2017. Published by Vladimir Semenko on his blog at Zavtra.ru, April 25, 2017, https://tinyurl.com/ydg5nwqg.

himself as an anti-ecumenist, antimodernist, and anti-Westernist. Chaplin and Druz' demonstrate that most political Orthodoxies are closely connected to each other, and their bottom line is warmongering. There were similar figures in the past who incarnated virtually all kinds of political Orthodoxies. For example, the Archbishop of Poltava Feofan Bystrov was an anti-Semite, antimodernist, anti-ecumenist, and monarchist.

Different political Orthodoxies in most cases appear together and support each other. However, sometimes they exclude one another. For instance, ethnic nationalism is often opposed to the civilizational version of nationalism. A conflict between ethnic and imperial (civilizational) versions of nationalism in the past led to the collapse of the empires. They continue colliding in the postimperial era. Both sorts of nationalism appeal to the church, and the church in many cases extends its support to them. This does not make them acceptable from the perspective of the gospel, which teaches us to love (Matt 19:19; 22:39; Mark 12:33) and not to hate our neighbor according to any version of nationalism. Although these nationalisms secure for the church a place in the public square, they distort the message that the church delivers in this square. This is a message that divides humankind into "us" and "them," and preaches "our" superiority to others.

There is a healthier alternative to both civilizational and ethnic nationalisms. It consolidates people not around common identities but around common civil values, such as solidarity and justice. Nationalism makes a people feel superior to other peoples. In contrast to this, the awareness that citizens in a civil society share urges them to treat others as their neighbors regardless of who and what they are. In this sense, unity of people based on civil values that apply to all humankind is closer to the gospel than the unity built on national or civilizational identities. Civil awareness is not common in the Orthodox milieu, which is occupied mostly by imperial or ethnic nationalisms. The Ukrainian Revolution of Dignity became an exception. The majority of those who gathered at the Maidan in Kyiv in the winter of 2013–2014 stood mostly for universal values of justice and solidarity. Only a minority of the protesters pursued an agenda of ethnic nationalism. In the aftermath of the Maidan, during the new elections for the Ukrainian Parliament, Verkhovna Rada, not a single nationalist party received seats. This contrasts sharply with many established democracies in Europe, where the nationalist parties in the same period dramatically increased their presence in parliaments.

Civil awareness is often criticized for its secular character and therefore is seen by the churches with suspicion. However, this is not a universal rule. The Ukrainian case has demonstrated that civil society can be born with the blessing of the church and can feature a strong religious dimension. Every day of protests at the Maidan, where the civil society was emerging, began and ended with common prayer. The square was filled with icons and quotes from the Bible. Most Ukrainian churches in return supported the Maidan and its demands. It became one of the rare cases when Orthodox churches endorsed not a national agenda but a civil one. These churches acknowledged civil society as their partner instead of their usual acknowledgement of either nation or state. The Maidan thus became a quantum leap in the development of the church's awareness from ethnic to civil. This development is important not only for the Ukrainian society but for the entire Orthodox world. It suggested a more orthodox alternative to the unorthodox Orthodoxy of nationalism.

The momentum of shifting from the political Orthodoxies of both ethnic and civilizational nationalisms, which was inspired by the Ukrainian Maidan and endorsed by the Ukrainian churches, was disrupted by the Russian aggression against Ukraine. The political regime of Vladimir Putin was afraid that the citizens of the Russian Federation would wake up to a similar reality as the citizens of Ukraine. The Maidan became a threat to the Russian kleptocratic and oppressive regime. To justify the aggression against Ukraine, Russian propaganda lied about the nature of the Maidan and misrepresented it as a manifestation of the Ukrainian nationalism. Although there were nationalist groups at the Maidan, they constituted a minority

there. The majority of the protesters were against violence and nationalist agendas of any sort. Lies about
the Maidan became one of the earliest instances of
post-truth—an imitation of truth that appeals to emo-
tions rather than reason.[4]

Post-truth occupies a central place in the ideology
of the Russian world, which has been constructed to
mobilize the Russian people for war. The Russian
Orthodox Church articulated this ideology, while the
Russian state enforced and delivered it, through media,
to many minds and souls in Russia and beyond. All
forms of political Orthodoxy were mobilized to this
end. Thus, the Russian world pretends to protect Russian civilization against the alleged assault from the
West. Its real purpose, however, is to protect Putin's
authoritarian kleptocracy, from which the church also
benefits. Fritz Morstein Marx compared totalitarian
ideology with a Leviathan (a sea monster referred to in
Job 3:8 and Ps 104:26), which functions similarly to the
church.[5] In the case of the Russian world, the church
has acted as a Leviathan. It produces an ideology that
attacks everything that resists the restoration of the
neo-Soviet empire.

The neo-Soviet ideology of the Russian world contains most forms of political Orthodoxies discussed in

---

4. See Cyril Hovorun, "Post-Truth," *Public Orthodoxy*, September 22, 2017,
https://tinyurl.com/y6vp942a.
5. F. Morstein Marx, "Totalitarian Politics," in *Symposium on the Totalitarian
State from the Standpoints of History, Political Science, Economics and Sociology, 17
November 1939*, (Philadelphia: American Philosophical Society, 1940), 2.

this book: it has become coercive, anti-Western, antimodernist, and antidemocratic. It tries to reanimate the Soviet past and to prevent the democratic modernization of society. It is excluding and threatening those who are not Russians or Orthodox: Ukrainians, Crimean Tatars, Jews, Protestants, and Greek Catholics, for example. The war in Ukraine has exacerbated and made all forms of political Orthodoxies violent: antimodernism, conservatism, and Occidentalism among other *-isms*. This has galvanized many ideologemes cherished by political Orthodoxies to strategemes—plans for military campaigns.

The ideology of the Russian world is a blend of modernism and postmodernism. On the one hand, it uses the power of the classical modernist ideologies, such as communism, fascism, and Nazism, to consolidate masses of people and drive them forward by means of propaganda and coercion. It has imported totalitarianism and civilizational nationalism from the twentieth to the twenty-first century. A central place in it is occupied not by a nation but an imagined civilization. In this regard, the Russian world is one of those "imagined communities" described by Benedict Anderson.[6] As an ideology, the Russian world does not reflect an empirical reality but resides in and captivates the imagination of a people. All these features make it a modernist phenomenon.

6. Benedict Anderson, *Imagined Communities: Reflections on the Origin and Spread of Nationalism* (London: Verso, 2006), 6.

On the other hand, in postmodern fashion it relativizes truth and generates post-truth. In the same fashion, it aligns historically incompatible figures such as Tsar Nikolai II Romanov and Iosif Stalin—two supreme deities in the temples of the Russian civil and political religion, respectively. The postmodern element of the Russian world can be also observed in the practices of reconstructing narratives. The protagonist of the military campaigns of the Russian world, Igor Girkin, who with Russian troops occupied the city of Sloviansk in the east of Ukraine in 2014, had been an actor who reconstructed the battles of the Romanov empire. He played an imperial Russian officer in reenacted battles. The game continued for him in Ukraine, this time with real blood being spilled. The Russian world, in this sense, is closer not to the models of civilizations penned by Samuel Huntington but to Sid Meier's video game, *Civilization*. Just as in the game there are distinct civilizations built around their own religions fighting each other due to differences, so the Russian world interprets itself as an Orthodox civilization that wrestles with the presumably Catholic, Protestant, and atheist liberal civilizations of the West. The Russian world thus is both modern and postmodern, and at the same time neither of them. I would call it postpostmodern, in the sense of synthesis of modernism and postmodernism as the next stage after postmodernism.

Many points of modern political Orthodoxies

coincide with the interests of the political regime of Vladimir Putin. This regime utilizes political Orthodoxies to promote and legitimize itself. It thus recruits many Christians worldwide as supporters—not only Russians and not only Orthodox. These Christians are unable to discern between the norms of gospel and the simulacra offered by political Orthodoxies. Even the Vatican and the World Council of Churches hesitated to acknowledge Russia's violence against Ukrainians, Tatars, Muslims, Catholics, and Protestants.[7]

More embarrassing is the silence of the Orthodox churches. They have not expressed any concern regarding the wars between Orthodox peoples: Russians and Georgians in 2008 and Russians and Ukrainians in 2014. Russian political and financial support for some churches made them silent about their Orthodox brethren being killed by other Orthodox who come in the name of the Russian world. A significant number of Orthodox hierarchs and theologians worldwide appear to favor the political Orthodoxies operating in the east of Ukraine. Particularly popular among the Orthodox is the anti-Western agenda of the Russian aggression against Ukraine.

It would be unfair to blame the Orthodox church for neglecting political Orthodoxies altogether. Some Orthodox churches have tackled some instances of it. Most famously, a council held in Constantinople in

7. See Cyril Hovorun, "Christian Duty in Ukraine," *First Things* 255 (July 2015): 21–23.

1872 condemned Balkan-style nationalism. At this council, civilizational Greek nationalism clashed with ethnic Bulgarian nationalism. Although this council apparently cohered with the political interests of the Ottoman empire, the importance of its decisions survived the empire itself.

The conflict between Bulgarian and Greek nationalisms began when the Bulgarian community in the territory of the Ottoman empire experienced an awakening of its national identity and looked for more political autonomy for itself. It saw the autonomization of its church from the patriarchate of Constantinople as an instrument through which to gain more political autonomy for the Bulgarian people. The Bulgarian movement, which consisted of ecclesial and political elements, began in the provinces with a Bulgarian majority, such as Tirnovo, and eventually arrived at Constantinople, where the large Bulgarian community had a high concentration of political and intellectual resources. The list of the Bulgarian demands included allowance for Bulgarian bishops, Bulgarian schools, and Bulgarian books for the Bulgarian communities. They also wanted the Bulgarian people to be represented directly at the High Porte, without the mediation of the patriarch of Constantinople as the head of the Orthodox *millet*. They also wanted to have a Bulgarian church in Constantinople.

The Ottoman government tried to accommodate some Bulgarian demands in the spirit of *Tanzimât*, the liberal reforms introduced by the sultans Mahmud II (1784–1839) and Abdülmecid I (1823–1861). The Greek community and the Russian embassy opposed these demands and made the Ecumenical patriarchate accept fewer of the Bulgarian demands than even the Ottoman authorities. The assembly of the Orthodox *millet*, gathered on the request of the Ottoman government and presided over by the patriarch of Constantinople, eventually allowed dioceses with a Bulgarian majority to have Bulgarian bishops. At the same time, the assembly rejected the bishops' election by the people, the use of the Slavonic language for liturgies, and the financial accountability of the dioceses to people.

In 1870, a draft of the *fermânı* (sultan's decree) envisioned establishing an independent Bulgarian church with the status of an exarchate and its own synod. This church, however, would have the patriarch of Constantinople as its spiritual leader and would commemorate him in the liturgies. The Greek community and the Ecumenical patriarchate did everything possible to prevent the signing of this decree. Therefore, it was put to action with some delay in 1872. As a result of the delay, the Bulgarian exarch Antim (1816–1888) proclaimed complete independence from the patriarchate of Constantinople. This decision corresponded to the Bulgarian struggle for complete independence from the Ottomans and thus went far beyond what the *fermânı* would allow.

The church of Constantinople used this excessive

Bulgarian action as an opportunity to counter-attack the Bulgarian movement toward independence. To deal with the Bulgarian issue, the patriarch convened a council in August 1872, which became a major Orthodox conciliar event of the nineteenth century. Several hierarchs from different Eastern churches attended this council, including ex-patriarchs of Constantinople, the patriarchs of Alexandria and Antioch, the archbishop of Cyprus, and some other metropolitans and bishops. The patriarch of Jerusalem initially attended the sessions of the council but then left before the final decision was adopted.

The council imposed an interdict on the entire Bulgarian church, which was lifted only in 1945. For seventy-three years, Constantinople and some other churches regarded this church as an "illegal gathering" (παρασυναγωγή). The Bulgarian church was formally accused of *phyletism* (φυλετισμός), which literally means "tribalism" and was defined by the council as an approach that brings "national distinctions" (φυλετικαὶ διακρίσεις) into the church and causes "controversies on ethnic grounds" (ἐθνικὴ ἔρις).[8] The language that the Patriarchate of Constantinople adopted in its official periodical was even stronger. *Ekklesiastiki Alithia* (Ἐκκλησιαστικὴ Ἀλήθεια ["Ecclesiastical Truth"]) characterized phyletism as a "Bulgarian heterodoxy" (βουλγαρικὴ κακοδοξία and ἑτεροδοξία) and

---

8. Published in the official periodical of the Ecumenical Patriarchate *Ekklisiastiki alithia* [Ecclesiastical Truth] 52 (1908): 554.

the "antichrist's doctrine" (ἀντιχριστιανικὴ διδασκα-λία).[9]

The council was not consistent in its decisions. On the one hand, it condemned nationalism as an ideology that divides the church. On the other hand, it condemned only ethnic nationalism. The council did not touch on civilizational nationalism. Besides this, the council's treatment of Bulgarian nationalism was not equal to its treatment of Greek nationalism, which earlier in the century led to the separation of the Greek church from Constantinople. The patriarchate did not recognize the Greek autocephaly for a while but never put the entire church under a ban.

The decisions of the council of 1872 can be also understood as condemning political interference in matters of faith, because the Bulgarian movement toward autocephaly was politically motivated. At the same time, the policies of Constantinople in the case of the Bulgarian national movement were also motivated politically: the church served the political ends of the Ottomans, who were against an independent Bulgarian state and church. Nevertheless, as inconsistent as it was, the council of 1872 became a milestone in dealing with political Orthodoxy. It created a precedent for more consistent decisions regarding the issue of nationalism.

More consistent in treating phyletism, or, as it was

9. *Ekklisiastiki alithia* [Ecclesiastical Truth] 52 (1908): 553.

189

also called, *ethnophyletism* (ἐθνοφυλετισμός), was the Panorthodox council, which was held in Crete in June 2016. This council had a broader agenda and was more representative than the council of 1872, though four local churches did not attend (the churches of Antioch, Russia, Georgia, and Bulgaria). The council affirmed the ecumenical character of the council in Constantinople in 1872. It also confirmed the condemnation of phyletism. However, the range of nationalisms tackled by the council in Crete was broader than in the case of the council of Constantinople: it implied condemnation not only of ethnic nationalism but also of its civilizational version. It is also noteworthy that the language of the council of 2016 regarding phyletism is harsher than the language of the council of 1872: the 2016 Panorthodox council called Phyletism "an ecclesiological heresy."[10]

The position of the church of Constantinople in 1872 could be interpreted as imperial because it aligned with the policies of the Ottoman Porte and the interests of Hellenic civilization. Therefore, the condemnation of phyletism in 1872 was effectively an attack of the imperial/civilizational nationalism against ethnic nationalism. In 2016, the Panorthodox council extended the notion of phyletism to both types of nationalisms: ethnic and civilizational. This is what

---

10. *Encyclical of the Holy and Great Council of the Orthodox Church* 3, https://tinyurl.com/y9yfk2hn.

was implied in the opening address by the Archbishop of Cyprus Chrysostomos II:

> In my opinion, the inter-Orthodox rivalries on account of ethnophyletism were the first reason why the preparations for the Council took so long. Ethnophyletism is what blocked the question of autocephaly and of the diptychs from coming to the Council, and is also the cause behind the less than canonical solution given to the issue of the diaspora. Nowadays, at a time when national barriers are being eliminated one after the other, we Orthodox do not just set ourselves at naught, but also set ourselves up for ridicule by setting up ethnicity as a constitutive element of our ecclesiology and our ecclesial identity.[11]

The church that blocks solutions to the issues of autocephaly and autonomy is the Moscow Patriarchate. This church is also a protagonist of civilizational nationalism. Therefore, by condemning the ethnophyletism that impedes solutions to important issues from the inter-Orthodox agenda, the archbishop of Cyprus obviously implied the standpoint of the Russian church. Ethnophyletism was also regarded by many at the Panorthodox council as a motivation for some churches not to come to Crete. In the case of the Russian church, this is civilizational nationalism, as mentioned above. For the Georgian and Bulgarian church,

11. "Address of His Beatitude Archbishop Chrysostomos of Cyprus to the Holy and Great Council," June 24, 2016, https://tinyurl.com/yb6osvkv. The Greek original of the speech published at https://tinyurl.com/y8vl74c4.

it is ethnic nationalism. That is why it is possible to assume that the Panorthodox council, by condemning ethnophyletism as reason for the absence of some churches, effectively targeted both versions of nationalism.

The Panorthodox council went another step further than the council of 1872. It condemned fundamentalism and violence on the basis of religion:

> We are experiencing today an increase of violence in the name of God. The explosions of fundamentalism within religious communities threaten to create the view that fundamentalism belongs to the essence of the phenomenon of religion. The truth, however, is that fundamentalism, as "zeal not based on knowledge" (Rom. 10:2), constitutes an expression of morbid religiosity. A true Christian, following the example of the crucified Lord, sacrifices himself and does not sacrifice others, and for this reason is the most stringent critic of fundamentalism of whatever provenance.[12]

The Panorthodox council deliberately avoided restricting religious violence and fundamentalism to other religions and thus acknowledged their existence in the Orthodox churches as well. The council, in effect, dealt with the violent outbursts of political Orthodoxies. Nevertheless, it did not tackle the phenomenon of political Orthodoxy as such. Another council tried to

---

12. *Encyclical of the Holy and Great Council of the Orthodox Church* 17, https://tinyurl.com/y9yfk2hn.

deal with this phenomenon on more fundamental premises. This was the council of bishops of the Ukrainian Orthodox Church (in union with the Moscow Patriarchate), which was held in December 2007. It actually used the term *political Orthodoxy* to denote the phenomenon of politicized religion: "We condemn the so-called 'political Orthodoxy,' which provisions bringing political slogans to the church."[13]

This decision was provoked by public processions in the central streets of Kyiv and other cities in Ukraine organized by pro-Russian Orthodox "brotherhoods." They called themselves "brotherhoods" but in fact were political groups using religious attributes to promote political agendas. At these processions, they carried icons and other religious symbols together with political slogans against, for instance, the integration of Ukraine into the European Union and NATO. These political groups, which presented themselves as religious, were sponsored by the Kremlin through different political organizations in Ukraine, such as the Communist Party of Ukraine. As well, the leadership of the Russian church encouraged the "brotherhoods" and supported them in many ways, including financially. The Ukrainian Orthodox Church nevertheless at that time opposed the "brotherhoods" and condemned

13. Protocol 2 of the council of bishops of the Ukrainian Orthodox Church, December 21, 2007, available on the official website of the UOC: https://tinyurl.com/ycyaydms. The author of this book drafted the decision of the council of 2007.

their political activities. Despite its focus on local issues, the council's decision is crucially important for the entire Orthodox oecumene. It was also an early warning about the imminent aggression of the Russian world. When Russia launched its aggression, some members of the "brotherhoods" joined separatist groups in the east of Ukraine with guns in hand. Thus, the political Orthodoxy condemned by the Ukrainian bishops proved to be a dangerous political program that made wars in twenty-first-century Europe possible.

The majority of the Orthodox churches nevertheless hesitate to condemn not only the Russian aggression against Ukraine but any crime in which the churches were involved. The most appalling crime committed with consent or even direct contribution of some Orthodox churches is the Holocaust. Because the churches refuse to acknowledge their role in this crime, anti-Semitism still frames the worldview of many Orthodox. They do not realize that anti-Semitism is not just a crime against humanity but also a heresy similar to ancient heretical doctrines. It is a distortion of Orthodox teaching about incarnation. In classical christological doctrine, God received the fullness of humanity to save all human beings. The humanity of the incarnated Logos remained unalienated and unseparated from the rest of humanity regardless of their race, gender, and social status. All major christological heresies of the past effectively

built a wall between God and humankind, thus imped-
ing the salvation of the latter. Arianism, for instance,
made the godhead of Jesus created, and in this way sep-
arated him from the uncreated Father. Nestorianism
made the humanity of Jesus a subject coexistent with
the subject of the Logos under the same appearance
of Jesus's face (*prosopon*). As a result, Jesus's humanity became separate from the rest of humankind. It
was only the individual being of Jesus who was saved
through the incarnation, not the rest of humanity. In
monophysitism,[14] the humanity of Jesus was alienated
and turned into something different from the rest of
humanity. The alienation of Christ's humanity thus
became a wall between God and humanity. In anti-
Semitism, the Jewishness of Jesus becomes a similar
wall between God and humanity. For anti-Semitic theologians, universal salvation cannot spring from a Jew;
that would be a "heresy." The anti-Semitic "Orthodoxy" holds that to be able to save humankind, Jesus
has to be stripped of his Jewishness. This "Orthodoxy,"
however, is a heresy from the perspective of classical
patristic theology: it alienates the humanity of Jesus
from what it actually is in a way similar to the original
monophysitism. Besides this, anti-Semitic Christology
interprets salvation not as deliverance from sins and

14. There is a difference between the original monophysitism associated with
the name of Archimandrite Eutyches (c. 380–c. 456) and the "monophysite"
identity misleadingly ascribed to the Oriental churches. What is being said
here regarding "monophysitism" applies to the former and does not apply
to the latter.

195

corruption common to every human being but from Jewishness. It identifies being a Jew with being sinful.

Anti-Semitism is based on an ontological rendering of the human condition. A capacity of a group of people (being Jewish, for instance) is given a distinct ontological status of having a different nature than the rest of people. The same idea underpins racism. According to the racist perception of humanity, skin color makes groups of people ontologically different from each other. Nationalists sometimes also see differences between nations as ontological and pertinent to human nature. A way out of anti-Semitism, racism, and nationalism would be regarding the entire human nature as common for every human being. Classical Orthodox Christology suggests such a way out: because the incarnation of the Son of God in the person of Jesus Christ was a universal ontological happening that embraced all human beings regardless of their race and ethnicity, racial and national differences between men and women are not ontological. They can be cultural or simply imagined but have no meaning from the perspective of the incarnation of God.

Anti-Semitism is heretical also because it distracts Christians from the person of Jesus Christ and effectively replaces him in their worldview with the figure of the antichrist. The antichrist can be found in the center of most forms of the Russian political Orthodoxy. Russian anti-Semites regard Jews as his epigones. Monarchists venerate the tsar as a mysterious figure mentioned by Paul: *katechon* (ὁ κατέχων)—one who restrains (2 Thess 2:7). They believe that the tsar restrains the kingdom of antichrist. Even in Ukraine, the pro-Russian separatists and Russian mercenaries fight against an imagined antichrist.[15] The paradox of the political Orthodoxies of this sort is that while fighting against an imagined antichrist, they welcome more real ones.

The final question that we need to answer is whether political Orthodoxies can be eliminated from the church completely. It seems unlikely that this may happen one day. The church has been experiencing their pressure since its early centuries. Among their early forms were coercion, hierarchism, and symphony, for example. The church eventually yielded to these forms of political Orthodoxies. It is unlikely that Orthodox Christianity will ever get rid of them altogether in any foreseeable future. This does not, however, mean that it should not tackle them. There is a firewall that helps protect the church from the political Orthodoxies: its separation from the state. Indeed, the politicization of religion was particularly strong in the era when the church and the state constituted a

15. In a video clip about the activities of the "Russian Orthodox Army" in the Donbas, a monk teaches the newly recruited soldiers why and how they should use their weapons: "Antichrist is coming to the Holy Rus'. What we're seeing now—it's primarily a spiritual war, because the Antichrist comes to Holy Russia, against Orthodoxy." "Russkaya Pravoslavnaya Armiya, iyul' 2014 g." [Russian Orthodox Army, July 2014], YouTube video, 8:22, uploaded by "Andrey Smirnov," July 23, 2014, https://tinyurl.com/ybqpknkq.

single theopolitical organism. This era was marked by a confused politico-ecclesial self-awareness. The state and the church did not think of themselves as separate from each other: the two consciousnesses were conflated. This led to the confusion of interests and methods that the state and the church applied in pursuing their goals. As a result, the church embarked on several political Orthodoxies, including coercion. This era of "symphonic," or rather symbiotic, relationship between the church and state was the longest in the history of Christianity and lasted from the times of Eusebius and Constantine to the times of Hobbes and Jefferson. Thomas Jefferson's (1743–1826) "wall" between the church and state marked a new era of separation between them.

The process of separation was painful for the church, which during the centuries of symbiosis with the state came to identify itself with the latter. The church often resisted, and in some cases still resists, the process of separation because it considers this process a threat. However, the church eventually benefited from such separation, for several reasons. First, the church regained its own self-awareness as different from the state. It realized its own interests and tasks do not always cohere with the tasks of the state. Second, the church relearned how to act in noncoercive ways. The church may still desire to apply force. However, without support of the state, the church cannot be coercive anymore, and this causes phantom pains in its body. This is an uncomfortable situation that nevertheless forces the church to return to its apostolic non-coercive ethos. Third, the church receives a protection circuit against political influences. The wall between the church and the state is effectively a firewall that protects the ecclesial system from the malicious political activities of the state. This firewall keeps the church safe from any remote control, as it were, the state or other political agencies might try to exert on it. This circuit protects the church from various forms of political Orthodoxy.

There is another circuit that can protect the church from political Orthodoxies: the church's own self-awareness as church. Indeed, the church becomes alienated from its nature and purpose when it allows its self-awareness to dissolve in various political agendas. This applies primarily to conservative political Orthodoxies, which are inspired by the alliance of the churches with the state. It also applies to liberal political Orthodoxies when the church substitutes the exclusively humanistic tasks of liberal societies for its salvific purposes. In both cases, the church ceases to understand itself as a subject different from other subjects: authoritarian state or liberal society. When the church regains its self-awareness, however, this preserves it from being assimilated into political agendas. The church's self-awareness as church keeps its transcendental reference uncompromised. The church then can resist self-imposed secularization. At the same time, this allows the church to participate in various social activities without being dissolved in them. The church then collaborates with the state or society as a partner, not as someone who has lost his or her identity and self-awareness.

The strongest medicine against political Orthodoxies is repentance. Not only individual Christians but also churches can and should repent. This does not go against the nature of the church. This nature is both divine and human. Its divine part does not need repentance, but its human part does. The church consists of human beings who sin. Members of the church can sin individually or collectively. The leadership of the church can sin as leadership. Therefore, the church can and should repent. Repentance is the only way for the human side of the church to comply with its divine side. Political Orthodoxies are an obstacle for the unity and coherence of the church's nature. To remove this obstacle, the church needs to acknowledge its sins and decide to get rid of them. Unrepented political Orthodoxies harden with the passage of time. Every decade and every century they penetrate deeper under the skin of the church's body, destroying its tissues. They intoxicate the body until they are removed through the surgery of repentance.

Political Orthodoxies distract the church from its original Orthodoxy—bringing people to God in the straight and unimpeded way. Deconstruction of false Orthodoxies is possible through the reconstruction of

Orthodoxy as the apostles and the fathers of the church taught and lived it. An alternative to the politicization of the church is the apostolic and patristic way of believing, behaving, and belonging.

Bibliography

Anderson, Benedict. *Imagined Communities: Reflections on the Origin and Spread of Nationalism.* London: Verso, 2006.

Applebaum, Anne. *Red Famine: Stalin's War on Ukraine.* New York: Doubleday, 2017.

Bell, Daniel. *The End of an Ideology: On the Exhaustion of Political Ideas in the Fifties.* New York: Collier, 1962.

Bellah, Robert N. *The Broken Covenant: American Civil Religion in Time of Trial.* Chicago: University of Chicago Press, 1992.

Bellah, Robert N., and Phillip Hammond. *Varieties of Civil Religion.* San Francisco: Harper & Row, 1980.

Berger, Peter. *The Sacred Canopy: Elements of a Sociological Theory of Religion.* Garden City, NY: Doubleday, 1967.

Berger, Peter, ed. *The Desecularization of the World: Resurgent Religion and World Politics.* Grand Rapids: Eerdmans, 1999.

Breuilly, John, ed. *The Oxford Handbook of the History of Nationalism.* Oxford: Oxford University Press, 2013.

Brubaker, Rogers. *Citizenship and Nationhood in France and Germany*. Cambridge, MA: Harvard University Press, 1992.

Brustein, William. *Roots of Hate: Anti-Semitism in Europe Before the Holocaust*. Cambridge: Cambridge University Press, 2010.

Demacopoulos, George, and Aristotle Papanikolaou, eds. *Orthodox Constructions of the West*. New York: Fordham University Press, 2013.

Gorski, Philip S. *American Covenant: A History of Civil Religion from the Puritans to the Present*. Princeton: Princeton University Press, 2017.

Gregor, A. James. *Totalitarianism and Political Religion: An Intellectual History*. Stanford: Stanford University Press, 2012.

Griffin, Roger, ed. *Fascism, Totalitarianism and Political Religion*. London: Routledge, 2005.

Hastings, Adrian. *The Construction of Nationhood: Ethnicity, Religion, and Nationalism*. Cambridge: Cambridge University Press, 1997.

Heschel, Susannah. *The Aryan Jesus: Christian Theologians and the Bible in Nazi Germany*. Princeton: Princeton University Press, 2010.

Hobsbawm, Eric J. *Nations and Nationalism since 1780: Programme, Myth, Reality*. Cambridge: Cambridge University Press, 1990.

Kellogg, Michael. *The Russian Roots of Nazism: White Émigrés and the Making of National Socialism, 1917-1945*. Cambridge: Cambridge University Press, 2008.

Klier, John, and Shlomo Lambroza, eds. *Pogroms: Anti-Jewish Violence in Modern Russian History*. Cambridge: Cambridge University Press, 2007.

Koundoura, Maria. *The Greek Idea: The Formation of National and Transnational Identities*. London: Tauris, 2007.

Leustean, Lucian N. *Orthodoxy and the Cold War*. New York: Palgrave Macmillan, 2009.

Leustean, Lucian N., ed. *Orthodox Christianity and Nationalism in Nineteenth-Century Southeastern Europe*. New York: Fordham University Press, 2014.

O'Meara, Dominic J. *Platonopolis: Platonic Political Philosophy in Late Antiquity*. Oxford: Oxford University Press, 2003.

Pelikan, Jaroslav. *Interpreting the Bible and the Constitution*. New Haven: Yale University Press, 2004.

Popa, Ion. *The Romanian Orthodox Church and the Holocaust*. Bloomington: Indiana University Press, 2017.

Rijt, Jan-Willem van der. *The Importance of Assent: A Theory of Coercion and Dignity*. Dordrecht: Springer, 2012.

Romocea, Cristian. *Church and State: Religious Nationalism and State Identification in Post-Communist Romania*. London: Continuum, 2011.

Shaw, Brent D. *Sacred Violence: African Christians and Sectarian Hatred in the Age of Augustine*. Cambridge: Cambridge University Press, 2011.

Sherratt, Yvonne. *Hitler's Philosophers*. New Haven: Yale University Press, 2014.

Snyder, Timothy. *Bloodlands: Europe between Hitler and Stalin*. New York: Basic Books, 2010.

Sugar, Peter F., ed. *Eastern European Nationalism in the Twentieth Century*. Lanham, MD: American University Press, 1995.

Taylor, Charles. *A Secular Age*. Cambridge, MA: Belknap Press of Harvard University Press, 2007.

Index